COMMITTEE ON EMBEDDING COMMON TEST ITEMS IN STATE AND DISTRICT ASSESSMENTS

DANIEL M. KORETZ (*Chair*), School of Education, Boston College; RAND Education, Washington, DC

SUSAN AGRUSO, Office of Assessment, South Carolina Department of Education

RONALD K. HAMBLETON, School of Education, University of Massachusetts, Amherst

H.D. HOOVER, Iowa Testing Programs, University of Iowa

BRIAN W. JUNKER, Department of Statistics, Carnegie Mellon University

JAMES A. WATTS, Southern Regional Educational Board, Atlanta, Georgia

KAREN K. WIXSON, School of Education, University of Michigan

WENDY M. YEN, CTB/McGraw-Hill, Monterey, California

REBECCA ZWICK, Graduate School of Education, University of California, Santa Barbara

PAUL W. HOLLAND, *Liaison*, Board on Testing and Assessment; Graduate School of Education, University of California, Berkeley

MERYL W. BERTENTHAL, *Study Director*

BERT F. GREEN, *Senior Technical Advisor*

JOHN J. SHEPHARD, *Senior Project Assistant*

THE NATIONAL ACADEMIES

National Academy of Sciences
National Academy of Engineering
Institute of Medicine
National Research Council

The **National Academy of Sciences** is a private, nonprofit, self-perpetuating society of distinguished scholars engaged in scientific and engineering research, dedicated to the furtherance of science and technology and to their use for the general welfare. Upon the authority of the charter granted to it by the Congress in 1863, the Academy has a mandate that requires it to advise the federal government on scientific and technical matters. Dr. Bruce M. Alberts is president of the National Academy of Sciences.

The **National Academy of Engineering** was established in 1964, under the charter of the National Academy of Sciences, as a parallel organization of outstanding engineers. It is autonomous in its administration and in the selection of its members, sharing with the National Academy of Sciences the responsibility for advising the federal government. The National Academy of Engineering also sponsors engineering programs aimed at meeting national needs, encourages education and research, and recognizes the superior achievements of engineers. Dr. William A. Wulf is president of the National Academy of Engineering.

The **Institute of Medicine** was established in 1970 by the National Academy of Sciences to secure the services of eminent members of appropriate professions in the examination of policy matters pertaining to the health of the public. The Institute acts under the responsibility given to the National Academy of Sciences by its congressional charter to be an adviser to the federal government and, upon its own initiative, to identify issues of medical care, research, and education. Dr. Kenneth I. Shine is president of the Institute of Medicine.

The **National Research Council** was organized by the National Academy of Sciences in 1916 to associate the broad community of science and technology with the Academy's purposes of furthering knowledge and advising the federal government. Functioning in accordance with general policies determined by the Academy, the Council has become the principal operating agency of both the National Academy of Sciences and the National Academy of Engineering in providing services to the government, the public, and the scientific and engineering communities. The Council is administered jointly by both Academies and the Institute of Medicine. Dr. Bruce M. Alberts and Dr. William A. Wulf are chairman and vice chairman, respectively, of the National Research Council.

The study was supported by Contract/Grant No. RJ97184001 between the National Academy of Sciences and the U.S. Department of Education. Any opinions, findings, conclusions, or recommendations expressed in this publication are those of the author(s) and do not necessarily reflect the view of the organizations or agencies that provided support for this project.

International Standard Book Number 0-309-06789-8

Additional copies of this report are available from:

National Academy Press
2101 Constitution Avenue NW
Washington, DC 20418
Call 800-624-6242 or 202-334-3313 (in the Washington Metropolitan Area).

This report is also available on line at http://www.nap.edu

Printed in the United States of America

Suggested citation: National Research Council (1999). *Embedding Questions: The Pursuit of a Common Measure in Uncommon Tests*. Committee on Embedding Common Test Items in State and District Assessments. D.M. Koretz, M.W. Bertenthal, and B.F. Green, eds. Board on Testing and Assessment, Commission on Behavioral and Social Sciences and Education. Washington, DC: National Academy Press.

BOARD ON TESTING AND ASSESSMENT

Acknowledgments

The Committee on Embedding Common Test Items in State and District Assessments wishes to thank the many people who helped to make possible the preparation of this report.

An important part of the committee's work was to gather data from research, policies, and practices on embedding. Many people gave generously of their time, at meetings and workshops of the committee and in interviews with committee staff.

The committee benefited tremendously from a presentation at its first meeting by Achieve, Inc. staff: Matthew Gandal, director of standards and assessment, Jennifer Vranek, senior policy analyst, and consultant David Wiley of Northwestern University. They provided the committee with a comprehensive overview of Achieve's efforts to develop a common national measure of student performance through embedding common items in state mathematics assessments.

At a committee workshop, Gordon M. Ambach, executive director of the Council of Chief State School Officers (CCSSO); Wayne H. Martin, director of the CCSSO State Education Assessment Center; and John R. Tanner, director of the Delaware Education Assessment and Analysis Office, offered local, state, and national perspectives on the purposes for which a common measure of student performance might be used. Don McLaughlin, chief scientist at the American Institutes of Research, and Michele Zimowski, senior survey methodologist at the

National Opinion Research Center of the University of Chicago, presented on-going research related to linking state mathematics assessments to the National Assessment of Educational Progress (NAEP). Michael Kolen, professor of education at the University of Iowa, discussed the inferences that educators and policy makers want to support with tests that produce individual scores and are linked to NAEP. Patricia Ann Kenney, research associate at the University of Pittsburgh's Learning Research and Development Center, presented her work on the content analysis of NAEP and demonstrated how differences in state content standards and assessments will affect the feasibility of embedding common NAEP items in uncommon tests. John Poggio, director of the Center for Educational Testing and Evaluation and professor of educational psychology and research at the University of Kansas, discussed Kansas' 1992 plan to embed NAEP items in the state testing program and why the plan was subsequently abandoned. Finally, Richard Hill, founder of the National Center for the Improvement of Educational Assessment, Inc., presented his study on the use of embedded NAEP items to estimate the rigor of Louisiana's performance standards relative to NAEP's. The committee is extremely grateful to all of these individuals who helped us clarify our thinking about many of the important issues surrounding our charge.

Other individuals provided information to the committee during small group discussions and telephone interviews. We are particularly grateful to Robert J. Mislevy, Educational Testing Service, and Eugene G. Johnson, American Institutes of Research, who gave us information about the NAEP marketbasket; Gage Kingsbury, research director of the Northwest Evaluation Association, who provided information about the NWEA item bank and locally developed tests; and Duncan MacQuarrie, Department of Curriculum and Assessment, Office of the Superintendent of Public Instruction, Washington State Department of Education, who provided us with information from the CCSSO State Collaborative on Assessment and Student Standards.

We owe a debt of gratitude to John Olson and Carl Andrews of CCSSO for providing the committee with important data about state testing programs. Without their help, and the help of Wayne Martin, we would not have been able to include the 1997-1998 school year information that is presented throughout this report.

We are especially grateful to Bert F. Green, who served as a consultant to the committee and provided invaluable assistance during all phases of the study. He worked tirelessly on our behalf, analyzing the issues, gathering data, and drafting chapters. The timely preparation of this report on an accelerated time schedule could not have happened without his dedication and contributions.

The Board on Testing and Assessment, under the leadership of Robert Linn, provided the committee with both guidance and support. We were particularly fortunate to have Paul W. Holland, professor of statistics at University of California at Berkeley and a member of the board, as a liaison member to this committee. As the chair of the Committee on Equivalency and Linkage of Educational Tests, Paul was well acquainted with the issues confronting us and proved to be a valuable guide and sounding board as we pondered the complexities of embedding.

We are very grateful to the professional staff of the Commission on Behavioral and Social Sciences and Education, without whose guidance, support, and hard work we could not have completed this report. Barbara B. Torrey, executive director of the commission and Michael J. Feuer, director of the Board on Testing and Assessment (BOTA), created staff support and resources whenever we needed them and provided guidance to us as we navigated through the various stages of completing a National Research Council study in a mere nine months. BOTA staff members Naomi Chudowsky and Karen Mitchell made major contributions to our work, attending committee meetings and discussing ideas with the committee and staff. Karen was particularly gracious in her willingness to read and comment on the many drafts of this report that we endlessly piled on her desk. BOTA staff members Alexandra Beatty and Robert Rothman also read and commented on early drafts of this report; the finished product is better for their efforts. We would be remiss if we didn't also thank two new members of the BOTA staff: Judith Koenig, study director of the Committee on NAEP Reporting Practices, for sharing her library of testing books and journals with us; and Richard Noeth, study director of the Committee on the Evaluation of the Voluntary National Tests, Year 2, for his guidance, support, and encouragement of our efforts.

John Shephard, although new to the Board, served unflappably and flawlessly as the committee's senior project assistant. He dealt smoothly with the logistics of our three committee meetings in four months, with our enormous collections and distributions of materials, and with a seemingly endless stream of text files, e-mail file attachments, and file revisions in incompatible word-processing formats. His assistance at critical junctures along the way made the creation of this report possible.

John received support when he needed it from other wonderful project assistants: Lisa Alston, Dorothy Majewski, Susan McCutchen, Kim Saldin, and Jane Phillips. Viola Horek, administrative associate to BOTA, was always there, instrumental in seeing that the entire project ran smoothly.

We are deeply grateful to Eugenia Grohman, associate director for reports of the Commission on Behavioral and Social Sciences and Education, for her advice on structuring the contents of the report and for her expert editing of the text. Genie knows better than anyone else how to put a report together, from beginning to end.

Above all, we thank the committee members for their outstanding contributions to the study. They drafted text, prepared background materials, and helped to organize workshops and committee discussions. Everyone contributed constructive, critical thinking, serious concern about the difficult and complex issues that we faced, and an open-mindedness that was essential to the success of the project.

This report has been reviewed in draft form by individuals chosen for their diverse perspectives and technical expertise, in accordance with procedures approved by the Report Review Committee of the National Research Council. The purpose of this independent review is to provide candid and critical comments that will assist the institution in making the published report as sound as possible and to ensure that the report meets institutional standards for objectivity, evidence, and responsiveness to the study charge. The review comments and draft manuscript remain confidential to protect the integrity of the deliberative process.

We thank the following individuals for their participation in the review of this report: Glenn Crosby, Department of Chemistry, Washington State University; John Guthrie, College of Education, University of Maryland; Lyle V. Jones, L.L. Thurstone Psychometric Laboratory, University of North Carolina, Chapel Hill; Stephen Raudenbush, School of Education, University of Michigan; Henry W. Riecken, Professor of Behavioral Sciences (emeritus), University of Pennsylvania School of Medicine; David Thissen, Graduate Program in Quantitative Psychology, University of North Carolina, Chapel Hill; Ewart A.C. Thomas, Department of Psychology, Stanford University; and Gary Williamson, Division of Accountability Services, North Carolina Department of Instruction, Raleigh.

Although the individuals listed above provided constructive comments and suggestions, it must be emphasized that responsibility for the final content of this report rests entirely with the authoring committee and the institution.

Meryl W. Bertenthal, *Study Director*
Daniel M. Koretz, *Chair*
Committee on Embedding Common
Test Items in State and District Assessments

Contents

Executive Summary

Policy makers are caught between two powerful forces in relation to testing in America's schools. One is increased interest on the part of educators, reinforced by federal requirements, in developing tests that accurately reflect local educational standards and goals. The other is a strong push to gather information about the performance of students and schools relative to national and international standards and norms. The difficulty of achieving these two goals simultaneously is exacerbated by both the long-standing American tradition of local control of education and the growing public sentiment that students already take enough tests.

Finding a solution to this dilemma has been the focus of numerous debates surrounding the Voluntary National Tests proposed by President Clinton in his 1997 State of the Union address. It was also the topic of a congressionally mandated 1998 National Research Council report (*Uncommon Measures: Equivalence and Linkage Among Educational Tests*), and was touched upon in a U.S. General Accounting Office report (*Student Testing: Issues Related to Voluntary National Mathematics and Reading Tests*).

More recently, Congress asked the National Research Council to determine the technical feasibility, validity, and reliability of embedding test items from the National Assessment of Educational Progress or other tests in state and district assessments in 4th-grade reading and 8th-grade mathematics for the purpose of developing a valid measure of student achievement within states and districts and in terms of national performance standards or scales. This report is the response to that congressional mandate.

CONCEPT AND PURPOSE OF EMBEDDING

Underlying the committee's discussion of embedding there are always two tests, which we identify as the "national test" and the "state test." The national test might be an actual test or testing program like the National Assessment of Educational Progress (NAEP) or one of the commercially available achievement tests, or it might be some other large pool of nationally calibrated test items. Performance on the national test items generates a "national score," the candidate for a common measure of individual student performance. The state test is whatever state or local testing program is already in place, and it produces a "state score" for students that is distinct from the national score. The goal of embedding is to produce both the national score and the state score without administering two full-length, free-standing tests.

Key to achieving that goal is the need for a common measure of student performance. A common measure is a single scale of measurement; scores from tests that are calibrated to this scale support the same inferences about student performance from one locality to another and from one year to the next. A given score indicates the same level of performance, no matter from which test or how the score was obtained. The scores might be obtained from a single test, from different tests that are calibrated to the same scale through linking, from extracts from a single test, or based on estimates of student performance from a matrix-sampled assessment.

Validity is the central criterion for evaluating any inferences based on test scores. When inferences about students' educational achievements are intended from test results, two things are critical: (1) the test must adequately sample the domain of knowledge and skills that the scores are supposed to represent, and (2) the test must always be administered under the same standardized conditions so that all test takers have the same opportunity to demonstrate what they know.

Developing a common measure of individual student performance by inserting an abridged test into the diversity of current state tests creates multiple opportunities for these two conditions to be violated, threatening the validity of most of the inferences that parents, educators, and policy makers want to support with test scores.

The type of embedding that the committee considered to be most central to its charge entails including parts of a national assessment in state assessment programs in order to provide individual students with national scores that are comparable to the scores that would have been obtained had they taken the national assessment in its entirety.

CONCLUSIONS

National scores that are derived from an embedded national test or test items are likely to be both imprecise and biased, and the direction and extent of bias is likely to vary in important ways—e.g., across population groups and across schools with different curricula. The impediments to deriving valid, reliable, and comparable national scores from embedded items stem from three sources: differences between the state and national tests; differences between the state and national testing programs, such as the procedures used for test administration; and differences between the embedded material and the national test from which it is drawn.

CONCLUSION 1: Embedding part of a national assessment in state assessments will not provide valid, reliable, and comparable national scores for individual students as long as there are: (1) substantial differences in content, format, or administration between the embedded material and the national test that it represents; or (2) substantial differences in context or administration between the state and national testing programs that change the ways in which students respond to the embedded items.

If the national assessment is administered in its entirety, close in time with a state assessment, and in a manner that is consistent with its standardization, many of the threats to comparability of national scores—such as context effects, differences in timing, and differences in administration—may be circumvented. In this situation, if state scores are not intended to be comparable across states, it does not matter that this approach may lead some states to administer their own test material differently than some other states. This approach is not without its limitations, however, and it can affect a state's testing programs in a variety of ways. State policy makers and educators must weigh the advantages, disadvantages, and tradeoffs that are associated with this approach.

CONCLUSION 2: When a national test designed to produce individual scores is administered in its entirety and under standard conditions that are the same from state to state and consistent with its standardization, it can provide a national common measure. States may separately administer custom-developed, state items close in time with the national test and use student responses to both the state items and selected national test items to calculate a state score. This approach provides both national and state scores for individual students and may reduce students' testing burdens relative to the administration of two overlapping tests.

The relative efficiency of embedding must be evaluated on a case-by-case basis and depends on many factors, including the length of the embedded test, required changes in administration practices at the state level, and differing regulations about which students are tested or excluded. States must weigh the costs and benefits that are associated with any embedding approach. However, differences in the time of year for testing, grades and subjects tested, content and format of the national and state tests, rules about assessment accommodations, the stakes associated with test results, and the uses and types of testing aids that are required and provided by different states create a situation that makes embedding items in state and district tests to derive a common measure of individual student performance both complex and burdensome.

CONCLUSION 3: Although embedding appears to offer gains in efficiency relative to administering two tests and does reduce student testing time, in practice, it is often complex and burdensome and may compromise test security.

The committee also considered other purposes for which embedding might be used to obtain aggregate information, i.e., scores of groups of students such as schools, districts, or states, rather than to obtain information about individual students. The extent to which embedding would provide valid estimates of aggregated scores on a national test that is not fully administered remains uncertain. Aggregation does lessen the effects of certain types of measurement error that contribute to the unreliability of scores for individual students. But many of the impediments to embedding are factors that vary systematically among groups, such as differences in rules for the use of accommodations (for students with disabilities or limited English proficiency) and differences in the contexts provided by state tests. Aggregation will not alleviate the distortions in the scores that are caused by these factors. Given the limited data available on this issue, the committee does not offer a conclusion about the use of embedding to obtain aggregate information.

1

Introduction: History and Context

Policy makers are caught between two powerful forces when it comes to testing in America's schools. One is the increased interest on the part of educators, reinforced by federal requirements, in developing tests that accurately reflect local educational standards and goals. The other is a strong policy push to gather information about the performance of students and schools relative to national and international standards and norms. The difficulty of simultaneously achieving these two goals is exacerbated by both the long-standing American tradition of local control of education and growing public sentiment that the nation's school children already face enough tests.

The search for a solution to this dilemma led Congress to request two separate studies from the National Research Council (NRC) to determine whether a common measure of student performance can be achieved by comparing or linking the results of different tests to each other and interpreting the results in terms of national or international benchmarks.

BACKGROUND

Despite significant state investments in standards and testing and in education generally, policy makers continue to look for clear evidence of how their states' students perform in comparison with students in other states and with national and international standards. The growing demand for national and international comparative achievement data is reflected in the growing public attention to results of such assessments as the National Assessment of Educational Progress (NAEP) and the Third International Mathematics and Science Study (TIMSS), but these programs do not provide individual student results.

National comparability of individual test results is difficult to attain. The United States does not have a national examination system that can show how an individual student's achievement compares with that of students in other schools, districts, and states. There is no uniform curriculum for each school subject or commonly accepted standards of academic performance. Instead, individual student achievement is currently measured by a variety of state-developed and commercially published tests.

State tests are designed to evaluate students, schools, and school districts with respect to state goals, but they do not provide information that is useful in making comparisons across states. Standardized commercial tests can provide information for making comparisons across states among students who take the same test, but they cannot provide a common measure of achievement for students who take different tests, even when these tests appear to be similar (National Research Council, 1999c).

Differences across states go deeper than the specific tests they choose to use, to the actual goals and standards for learning in each subject area. There is no national consensus, for example, on exactly what constitutes the subject areas of 4th-grade reading and 8th-grade mathematics, nor on what mathematical skills an 8th-grade student ought to have mastered, nor on what constitutes reading and writing competence of a 4th-grade student. Thus, different tests that ostensibly measure the same broad subject area can produce varying scores for the same students because the tests may emphasize different aspects of the subject area, such as algebra, computation, or graphical representation for 8th-grade mathematics. The lack of a readily available, nationally accepted "common currency" for describing and comparing individual student achievement leaves policy makers wondering what they can tell students and their families about how local students are performing relative to other students in the nation.

The first NRC study addressed the question of the feasibility of developing an equivalency scale that would allow test scores from commercially available standardized tests and state assessments to be compared with each other and NAEP. The linkage study (National Research Council, 1999c) concluded that state assessments and commercial tests are too diverse to be meaningfully linked to a single common scale and that reporting student scores from different assessments on the same scale is therefore not feasible. Although some of the measures might be sufficiently similar in content and format to be linked, the study concluded that differences in administrative practices and test uses would limit the valid inferences that might be drawn about individual students. The study also concluded that linking an existing test or assessment to the NAEP scale is problematic unless the test to be linked to NAEP is very similar in content, format, and uses to NAEP.

Policy makers accepted the report's conclusions, but the pressure to find ways to address the divergent goals of score comparability and local control of education did not disappear. In continuing to seek a viable means of deriving a common measure of student performance, and to do so efficiently, policy makers responded to the NRC report with several follow-up questions:

- Is there a way to combine elements of two different tests and get meaningful results for both?
- Can NAEP items or items from other nationally standardized tests simply be embedded in state tests in order to provide information related to national standards?
- Can one "sprinkle" a few items from one test in another test and lift the results out separately?
- Can one test be "attached" to or "contained within" another test?
- Are tests similar enough that common items can be found and used for different purposes at the same time?

At the same time that the NRC's linkage study was under way, preliminary work by Achieve, Inc., an independent policy organization, indicated widespread interest in trying to find strategies to answer those questions (Kronholz, 1998; Hoff, 1998).[1] After the NRC report, the notion of embedding items from one test in another to develop a common measure of student performance was thrust even more into the spotlight

---

[1] After careful consideration of the issues surrounding the selection of items to be used for embedding and the potential technical and practical difficulties associated with embedding the identified items in differing state tests, Achieve abandoned its attempt to develop such strategies (Achieve, Inc., personal communication, March 13, 1999; Hoff, 1999).

as a possible solution to the dilemma of score comparability with only a limited additional testing burden placed on the states.

In response, the Committee on Embedding Common Test Items in State and District Assessments was charged specifically (under P.L. 105-277) with examining research and practice to determine whether embedding NAEP or other items in state and district tests of 4th-grade reading and 8th-grade mathematics is a technically feasible way of obtaining a valid and reliable common measure of individual student performance.

COMMITTEE'S APPROACH

In accepting its charge, the committee acknowledged that the questions posed to it are important ones that reflect policy makers' keen desire for nationally comparable student achievement measures that can be developed without adding additional testing burdens to state programs. Therefore, in conducting its deliberations, the committee used the ability to achieve comparability with efficiency as one criterion for evaluating different strategies for embedding items to develop a common measure of individual student performance.

The committee made the assumption that the possibility of linking or embedding items in existing tests was being proposed as an alternative to the Voluntary National Tests (VNT) of 4th-grade reading and 8th-grade mathematics that were requested by President Clinton in his 1997 State of the Union address to Congress. While the committee takes no position on the overall merits of the VNT, it acknowledges that some of its findings and conclusions may be relevant to the technical and policy issues surrounding the tests.

The committee began by reviewing and accepting the evidence, conclusions, and relevance of two earlier related reports to Congress: *Uncommon Measures: Equivalence and Linkage Among Educational Tests* (National Research Council, 1999c) and *Student Testing: Issues Related to Voluntary National Mathematics and Reading Tests* (U.S. General Accounting Office, 1998). Because the committee accepted the conclusions of *Uncommon Measures* regarding the issues surrounding equating and linking, the committee focused its deliberations on the use of embedded items to develop a common measure that is not derived from linking or equating.

Although the congressional conference agreement (U.S. Congress, 1998) that elaborated the committee's charge specifically states that, ". . . including items from one test in another test for the purpose of providing a common measure of individual student performance is, effectively, a form of linking . . ," the committee considered the full range of embedding techniques, including some that do not entail statistical linking. The committee deliberated about the ways in which using embedding to develop a common measure of student achievement are the same as or different from linking.

Definitions

To facilitate its discussions, the committee formalized several key definitions and developed three scenarios of ways in which embedding could be implemented.

Embedding

Embedding is the inclusion of all or part of one test in another. In this report, however, embedding refers only to the inclusion of part of a test in another, since embedding all of a test offers no gains in efficiency over administering two tests separately. Accordingly, the focus of this report is a discussion of methods of embedding that entail varying degrees of abridgment of either the test from which embedded material is drawn or the test into which another test is embedded. There are tradeoffs imposed by the method and degree of abridgment—how the embedded material is selected from the entire test and how much of the entire test is included. For example, embedding larger amounts of material is likely to increase the reliability of scores, but at the cost of increasing the testing burden.

Underlying our discussion of embedding there are always two tests, which we call the "national test" and the "state test." The national test might be an actual test or testing program like NAEP or one of the commercially available achievement tests, or it might be some other large pool of nationally calibrated test items. In either case, performance on the national test items generates a "national score," the candidate for a common measure of individual student performance. The "state test" is whatever state or local testing program is already in place, and it produces a "state score" for students that is distinct from the national score.

The goal of embedding is to produce both a national score and a state score without administering two full-length, free-standing tests. Of course, embedding could take other forms, and the issues raised here would apply to them as well. However, because of NAEP's design, embedding NAEP material raises additional concerns (detailed in Chapter 2).

Two methods of embedding are included in our analysis: physical and conceptual. Physical embedding entails inserting material from the national test into a state's test booklets, either as a separate section of the state test or sprinkled throughout the state test. Conceptual embedding requires that the material from the national test be administered separately but close in time to the state test. Most of the embedding issues that the committee discusses arise in both cases, but conceptual embedding can be less subject to context effects (discussed in Chapter 2).

A Common Measure

The committee was charged with examining the usefulness of embedding items in state and district tests for the purpose of providing a common measure of individual student performance. But what is a "common measure?"

A common measure is a single scale of measurement; scores from tests that are calibrated to this scale support the same inferences about student performance from one locality to another and from one year to the next. To provide a common measure, tests must conform to technical standards (American Educational Research Association et al., 1985; American Educational Research Association et al., in press) and must meet a number of additional criteria, some of which are discussed below. In addition, it should be noted that even tests that provide a common measure may differ in reliability—that is, scores from one may be more precise than scores from another.

A given score indicates the same level of performance, no matter from which test or how the score was obtained. The score might come from performance on a single test, from different tests that are calibrated to the same scale through linking, from extracts from a single test, or from estimates of student performance from a matrix-sampled assessment.

A common measure does not necessarily imply a common or shared test. Common measures can be obtained from a common test that is always administered under standardized conditions, but they need not be. The motivation for this study, and for the study of linking reported in *Uncommon Measures*, is a widespread interest in obtaining comparable information about student performance without a common test: that is, without administering a full, common test in different states. *Uncommon*

Measures (National Research Council, 1999c) explored whether linking could provide a common measure from different tests when no common test is used at all. This study explores whether embedding might serve that function—in particular, embedding parts of a common test into different state or district tests.

Three Scenarios

To make the issues we raise more concrete, we developed three specific scenarios around which we organize our discussion about embedding for a common measure of individual performance (discussed in Chapter 3). We use the administration of two free-standing tests (discussed in Chapter 2) as a standard with which to compare the three embedding scenarios. Although we believe that these three scenarios illustrate the most likely approaches to embedding, they do not represent an exhaustive inventory of embedding techniques:

1. Double-duty scenario: In this scenario, a national test is administered independently of a state test, but some or all of the items from the national test are used with the state items in developing students' state scores.
2. NAEP-blocks scenario: In this scenario, NAEP item blocks, which have been chosen to represent the complete NAEP assessment to some degree, are inserted into a state test booklet.
3. Item-bank scenario: In this scenario, a national item bank is made available to local educational agencies, and state educators select the items they wish to use and embed them in their state tests.

Details about the design, analysis, and reporting for these scenarios are presented in Chapter 3, along with an evaluation of their technical quality for the purpose of producing a common measure of individual student performance. Our evaluation of these scenarios illustrates the advantages, disadvantages, and tradeoffs that are inherent in any proposal for creating a common measure through embedding.

Broader Issues

Although we focus mostly on whether a common measure of individual performance can be developed by embedding all or part of a test in another test, we identified a variety of other purposes for which policy makers may want a common measure of student performance, and we expanded our deliberations to consider them. They include: to report national test results from NAEP or other tests at the district or school level, to verify the level of rigor of local standards, to report NAEP results in non-NAEP administration years, and to audit changes in local test results over time. Because these purposes involve comparisons of group performance, aggregated scores (scores representing a group of individuals, such as a school, district, or state) would be more useful than individual scores. We note some important attributes of these alternatives, but we did not deliberate about them at length. Chapter 4 reports our limited findings and conclusions about these other purposes for embedding.

Some of the conclusions contained in this report reflect the current diversity of state curricula and tests. If the goals and characteristics of state testing programs were to become markedly more similar than they currently are, some of the obstacles to embedding noted here would be ameliorated to some degree. However, recent developments do not suggest that this is likely to happen in the near future. In addition, we note that the impediments to successful embedding noted here vary considerably in terms of their tractability. Some of them could be surmounted by simple decisions about the operation of state testing programs, while others cannot be overcome without fundamental changes in curriculum and assessment.

2

Environment for Embedding: Technical Issues

This chapter describes a number of issues that arise when embedding is used to provide national scores for individual students. In keeping with Congress's charge, we focus our attention primarily on embedding as a means of obtaining individual scores on national measures of 4th-grade reading and 8th-grade mathematics. The issues discussed here would arise regardless of the grade level or subject area, although the particulars would vary.

SAMPLING TO CONSTRUCT A TEST[1]

To understand the likely effects of embedding, it is necessary to consider how tests are constructed to represent subject areas. For present purposes, a key element of this process is sampling. A national test represents a sample of possible tasks or questions drawn from a subject area, and the material to be embedded represents a sample of the national test.

Tests are constructed to assess performance in a defined area of knowledge or skill, typically called a domain. In rare cases, a domain may be

[1]This material is a slight revision of a section of *Uncommon Measures* (National Research Council, 1999c:12-14)

small enough that a test can cover it exhaustively. For example, proficiency in one-digit multiplication could be assessed exhaustively in the space of a fairly short test. As the domain gets larger, however, this becomes less feasible. Even final examinations, administered by teachers at the end of a year-long course, cannot cover every possible content or skill area covered by the curriculum. Many achievement tests—including those that are especially germane to the committee's charge—assess even larger, more complex domains. For example, the NAEP 8th-grade mathematics assessment is intended to tap a broad range of topics that includes a wide variety of mathematical skills and knowledge that students should (or might) master over the course of their first 8 years in school. The assessment therefore includes items representing a variety of different types of skills and knowledge, including numbers and operations, measurement, geometry, algebra and functions, and data analysis and statistics. Commercial achievement test batteries cover equally broad content, as do state assessments.

Because the time available to assess students is limited, wide-ranging tests can include only small samples of the full range of possibilities. Performance on the test items themselves is not as important as is the inference it supports about mastery of the broader domains the tests are designed to measure. Missing 10 of 20 items on a test of general vocabulary is important not because of the 10 words misunderstood, but because missing one-half of the items justifies an inference about a student's level of mastery of the thousands of words from which the test items were sampled.

In order to build a test that adequately represents its domain, a number of decisions must be made. It is helpful to think of four stages leading to a final test: domain definition, framework definition, test specification, and item selection (see Figure 2-1). The choices made at each stage reduces the number of content and skills areas that will be directly sampled by the completed test.

First, the developers of an assessment define the scope and extent of the subject area, called the domain, being assessed. For example, the domain of 8th-grade mathematics includes not only material currently taught in (or by) the 8th grade, but also material that people think ought to be taught. During domain definition, decisions such as whether data analysis and statistics should be tested in the 8th grade would also be made.

To define the framework, the domain definition must be delineated

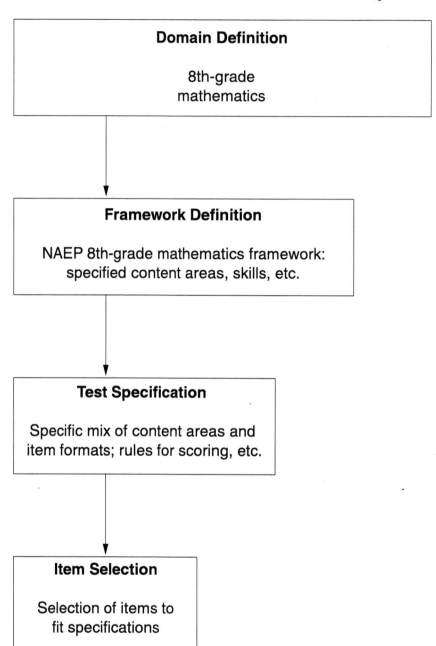

FIGURE 2-1 Decision stages in test development.

in terms of the content to be included, and the processes that students must master in dealing with the content. The NAEP 8th-grade mathematics framework represents choices about how to assess achievement in the content of 8th-grade mathematics. It identifies conceptual understanding, procedural knowledge, and problem solving as facets of proficiency and whether basic knowledge, simple manipulation, and understanding of relationships are to be tested separately or in some context.

Choices made at the next stage, test specification, outline how a test will be constructed to represent the specified content and skills areas defined by the framework. Test specifications, which are aptly called the test blueprint, specify the types and formats of the items to be used, such as the relative number of selected-response items and constructed-response items. Designers must also specify the number of tasks to be included for each part of the framework. Some commercial achievement tests, for example, place a much heavier emphasis on numerical operations than does NAEP. Another choice for a mathematics test is whether items can be included that are best answered with the use of a numerical calculator. NAEP includes such items, but the Third International Mathematics and Science Survey (TIMSS), given in many countries around the globe, does not. The NAEP and TIMSS frameworks are very similar, yet the two assessments have different specifications about calculator use.

Following domain definition, framework definition, and test specification, the final stage of test construction is to obtain a set of items for the test that match the test specification. These can come from a large number of prepared items or they can be written specifically for the test that is being developed. Newly devised items are often tried out in some way, such as including them in an existing test to see how the items fare alongside seasoned items. Responses to the new trial items are not included in the score of the host test. Test constructors evaluate new items with various statistical indices of item performance, including item difficulty, and the relationship of the new items to the accompanying items.

COMMON MEASURES FROM A COMMON TEST

To clarify the distinction between common tests and common measures, and to establish a standard of comparison for embedding, we begin our discussion of methods for obtaining individual scores on a common measure with an approach that entails neither linking nor embedding, but rather administration of an entire common national test and an entire state test.

Two Free-Standing Tests

In this situation, two free-standing tests are administered without any connection to each other. The national test is administered in its entirety under standardized conditions that are consistent from state to state: students in each state are given the same materials, the same directions, the same amount of time to complete the test, and so on. The combination of a common national test and common, standardized conditions of administration can yield a common measure of individual student performance, but at the cost of a substantial increase in burden (in time, money, and disruption of school routines) relative to the administration of a single state test.

The success of this approach hinges not only on the use of a common test, but also on standardization of administration and similarity in the uses of the scores. If test administration is not consistent from one location to another, for example, across states, even the use of a full common test may not guarantee a common measure. Moreover, when the national measure provides norms based on a standardization sample, the administration of the test must conform to the administration procedures used in the standardization.

However, even standardized administration procedures are not sufficient to guarantee a common measure. For example, suppose that two states administer an identical test and use similar procedures for administering the test, but use the scores in fundamentally different ways: in one state, scores have serious consequences for students as a minimum requirement for graduation; in another state, the scores have no consequences for students and are not even reported to parents, but are used to report school performance to the public. This difference in use could cause large differences in student motivation, and students in the second state may not put much effort into the test. As a result, identical scores in the two states might indicate considerably different levels of mastery of the content the test represents. Regardless of which of the two conditions (high or low motivation) produces more accurate scores, the scores will not be comparable. When scores are different for reasons other than differences in student achievement, comparisons based on scores are problematic.

Reconciling Scores

Two free-standing tests provide two scores for individual students: a state score and a national score. Because the state and national tests differ, the information from these scores would be different. That is, some students would do better on one test than on the other. Some of these differences could be large. Having two scores that are sometimes discrepant could be confusing to parents and policy makers. One can easily imagine, for example, complaints from the parent of a student who scored relatively poorly on a high-stakes state test but well on a low-stakes free-standing national test.

Yet, when two tests differ, they may provide different and perhaps complementary information about students' performance. Measurement experts have long warned against reliance on any single measure of student achievement because all measures are limited and prone to errors. The information about a student gathered from the results of two different well-constructed tests of a single domain would in general be more complete and more revealing than that from a single test (National Research Council, 1999b; American Educational Research Association et al., 1985; American Educational Research Association et al., in press).

One key to whether information from two tests would be seen as confusing or helpful is the care with which conclusions are presented and inferences drawn. If users treat scores of an 8th-grade mathematics test, for example, as synonymous with achievement in 8th-grade mathematics, differing results are likely to be confusing. But if users treat scores as different indications of mastery of that domain, the possibility exists for putting discrepancies among measures to productive use. An important caveat, however, is that in some cases, scores on one or the other test could be simply misleading—for example, if the student was ill the day it was administered.

With two free-standing tests another issue is inevitably raised: How fair are comparisons based on this approach? The committee noted that the fairness or reasonableness of a comparison hinges on the particular inferences the test scores are used to support. For example, suppose that two states agree to administer an identical mathematics test in the spring of the 8th grade. The test emphasizes algebra. In one state, most students study algebra in the 8th grade. In the second state, however, most students are not presented with this material until the 9th grade, and the corresponding instructional time is allocated instead to basic probability and data analysis, which is given almost no weight in the test. Because the test is more closely aligned with the curriculum in the first state than in the second, students in the first state will have an advantage on the test, all other things being equal.

Under these circumstances, when would it be fair to conclude that a given student in the second state is doing poorly, relative to students in the first state? If one were simply interested in whether students have mastered algebra and hazarded no speculation about why, it might be reasonable to conclude that the student is doing poorly. The student would in fact know less algebra than many students in the first state, if only because he or she had not been given the opportunity to learn algebra. But, if one wanted to draw inferences about a student's mastery of the broad subject area of mathematics, it might be unreasonable and misleading to infer from the results of this test, that the student in the second state is doing poorly relative to students in the first state.

THREATS TO OBTAINING A COMMON MEASURE

The use of a free-standing common test is in itself insufficient to guarantee comparability. We briefly note here some of the issues that arise when a common test is used to generate common scores. We present this material not to evaluate the two free-standing tests approach, but rather to provide a baseline for comparing the use of embedding. We also discuss these factors in relation to actual state policy and testing programs, with an emphasis on the ways in which differences among these programs can affect the comparability of results.

Standardization of Administration

To make fair and accurate comparisons between test results earned by students in different districts or states, or between students in one district or state and a national sample of students, tests must be administered under standardized conditions, so that the extraneous factors that affect student performance are held constant. For example, instructions to the examinees, the amount of time allowed, the use of manipulatives or testing aids, and the mechanics of marking answers should be the same for all students.

However, because of the expense involved in hiring external test administrators, most state tests are administered by the regular school staff, teachers, counselors, etc. Test administration usually means that

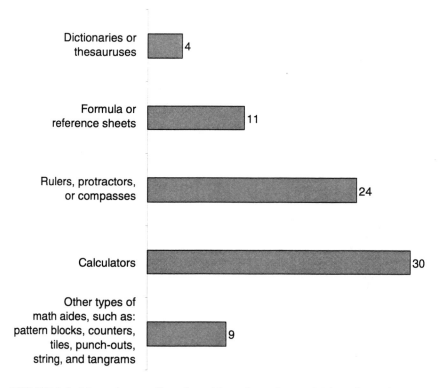

FIGURE 2-2 Manipulatives allowed on 4th-grade reading and 8th-grade mathematics components; number of states. SOURCE: Adapted from Olson et al. (in press).

the staff read the instructions for completing the test to the examinees from a script, which is designed to ensure that all students receive the same instructions and the same amount of time for completing the test. If all of the test administrators adhere to the standardized procedures, there is little cause for concern. There has been some concern expressed, however, by measurement specialists that teachers may vary in how strictly they adhere to standardized testing procedures (see, e.g., Kimmel, 1997; Nolen et al., 1992; Ligon, 1985; Horne and Garty, 1981).

If different states provide different directions for the national test, different opportunities to use calculators or manipulatives (see Figure 2-2), impose different time limits for students, or break the test into a different number of testing sessions, seemingly comparable scores from different states may imply different levels of actual proficiency.

Accommodations

One of the ways in which the standardized procedures for administration are deliberately violated is in the provision of special accommodations for students with special needs, such as students with disabilities or with limited proficiency in English. Accommodations are provided to offset biases caused by disabilities or other factors. For example, one cannot obtain a valid estimate of the mathematics proficiency of a blind student unless the test is offered either orally or in Braille. Other examples include extra time (a common accommodation), shorter testing periods with additional breaks, and use of a scribe for recording answers; see Table 2-1 for a list of accommodations that are used in state testing programs.

Two recent papers prepared by the American Institutes for Research (1998a, 1998b) for the National Assessment Governing Board summarize much of the research on inclusion and accommodation for limited-English-proficient students and for students with disabilities. However, information about the appropriate uses of accommodations for many types of students is unclear, and current guidelines for their use are highly inconsistent from state to state (see, e.g., National Research Council, 1997).

Differences in the use of accommodations could alter the meaning of individual scores across states, and the lack of clear evidence about the effects of accommodations precludes taking them into account in comparing scores (see, e.g., Halla, 1988; Huesman, 1999; Rudman and Raudenbush, 1996; Whitney and Patience, 1981; Dulmage, 1993; Joseph, 1998; Williams, 1981).

Timing of Administration

The time of year at which an assessment is administered will have potentially large effects on the results (see Figure 2-3 for a comparison of state testing schedules). The nature of students' educational growth in different test areas is different and uneven throughout the school year (Beggs and Hieronymus, 1968). In most test areas, all of the growth occurs during the academic school year, and in some areas students actually regress during the summer months (Cooper et al., 1996).

The best source of data documenting student growth comes from the national standardizations of several widely used achievement batteries. These batteries place the performance of students at all grade levels

TABLE 2-1 Accommodations Used by States

Type of Accommodation Allowed	Number of States
Presentation format accommodations	
Oral reading of questions	35
Braille editions	40
Use of magnifying equipment	37
Large-print editions	41
Oral reading of directions	39
Signing of directions	36
Audiotaped directions	12
Repeating of directions	35
Interpretation of directions	24
Visual field template	12
Short segment testing booklet	5
Other presentation format accommodations	14
Response format accommodations	
Mark response in booklet	31
Use of template for recording answers	18
Point to response	32
Sign language	32
Use of typewriter or computer	37
Use of Braille writer	18
Use of scribe	36
Answers recorded on audiotape	11
Other response format accommodations	8
Test setting accommodations	
Alone, in study carrel	40
Individual administration	23
With small groups	39
At home, with appropriate supervision	17
In special education class	35
Separate room	23
Other test setting accommodations	10
Timing or scheduling accommodations	
Extra testing time (same day)	40
More breaks	40
Extending sessions over multiple days	29
Altered time of day	18
Other timing-scheduling accommodations	9
Other accommodations	
Out-of-level testing	9
Use of word lists or dictionaries	13
Use of spell checkers	7
Other	7

SOURCE: Adapted from Roeber et al. (1998).

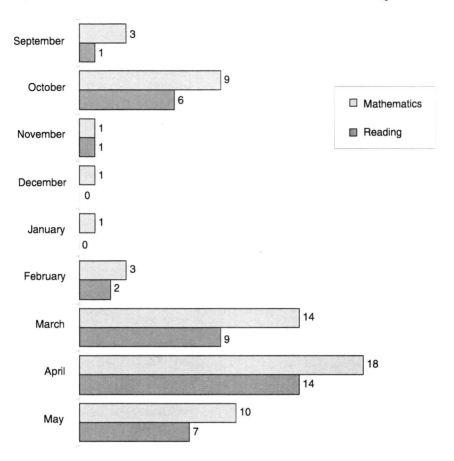

FIGURE 2-3 Time of administration of 4th-grade reading and 8th-grade mathematics components during the 1997-1998 school year; number of states. NOTES: States were counted more than once when their assessment programs contained multiple reading or mathematics components that were administered at different times during the year. SOURCE: Adapted from Olson et al. (in press).

(K-12) on a common scale, making it possible to estimate the amount of growth occurring between successive grade levels.[2]

The effect that time of year for testing could have on the absolute level of student achievement is illustrated in Table 2-2. This table shows

---

[2] The most recent national standardizations of the Stanford Achievement Test (SAT), the Comprehensive Tests of Basic Skills (CTBS), and the Iowa Tests of Basic Skills (ITBS)/Iowa Tests of Educational Development (ITED) showed very similar within-

the average proficiency in reading on the grade 4 1998 NAEP assessment for 39 states, the District of Columbia, and the Virgin Islands. If one were to assume the average within-grade growth for reading,[3] a difference of 3 months—the size of the testing window for NAEP—in the time of year when the test is administered could have up to a 16-point effect on the average proficiency level of a state or district. For illustration, 16 points is the difference in performance between the state ranked 5th (Massachusetts) and the state ranked 31st (Arkansas). A difference in testing time as small as 3 months could lead to changes in state ranking by as many as 26 places.

Some national assessments have norms for only one testing period per grade. NAEP, TIMSS, and the proposed VNT are examples of such tests. If one of these tests is selected to serve as a freestanding test or as the source for the embedded items, the state tests would have to be administered during the same testing period as the national assessment. Other tests, such as most commercially available, large-scale achievement tests, have norms available for various testing periods per grade. With these assessments, testing dates are flexible, and if they are the source for the embedded test, the national test can be administered during a time period that is most suitable for the local situation.

One additional issue that is related to the time of year for testing falls under the umbrella of "opportunity to learn." For example, if the same test is given at the same time of the year in different states that follow different curricula, or if the same test is given at different times of the year in states that follow the same curricula, students will not have had equal opportunities to learn the material before testing. For example, if reading and analyzing poetry is covered early in the school year in one state and covered after the assessment is given in another, test items that include reading poetry might be easier for students from the first state than for

---

grade growth [see CTB/McGraw Hill (1997), Feldt et al. (1996), Harcourt Brace Educational Measurement (1997), and Hoover et al. (1996)]. Expressed in a common metric of the within-grade standard deviation for students, the average annual growth in reading comprehension, averaged over the SAT, CTBS, and ITBS/ITED, was +.41, +.27, and +.14 SD units at grades 4, 8, and 11, respectively. In mathematics the values at the corresponding grade levels were +.61, +.30, and +.13.

[3]On this assessment, the within-grade standard deviation was 38 points on the NAEP proficiency scale. The average within-grade growth for grade 4 mathematics of +.41 SD units reported earlier indicates that the time of year of testing could have up to a 16-point effect ($38 \times +.41$) on the average proficiency level of a state or district.

TABLE 2-2 State Rankings from the 1998 NAEP 4th-Grade Reading
Assessment

Rank	State	Score
1	Connecticut	232
2	Montana	226
3	New Hampshire	226
4	Maine	225
5	Massachusetts	225
6	Wisconsin	224
7	Iowa	223
8	Colorado	222
9	Kansas	222
10	Minnesota	222
11	Oklahoma	220
12	Wyoming	219
13	Kentucky	218
14	Rhode Island	218
15	Virginia	218
16	Michigan	217
17	North Carolina	217
18	Texas	217
19	Washington	217
20	Missouri	216
21	New York	216
22	West Virginia	216
23	Maryland	215
24	Utah	215
25	Oregon	214
26	Delaware	212
27	Tennessee	212
28	Alabama	211
29	Georgia	210
30	South Carolina	210
31	Arkansas	209
32	Nevada	208
33	Arizona	207
34	Florida	207
35	New Mexico	206
36	Louisiana	204
37	Mississippi	204

TABLE 2-2 Continued

Rank	State	Score
38	California	202
39	Hawaii	200
40	District of Columbia	182
41	Virgin Islands	178

NOTE: This table illustrates the effect that a 3-month difference in test administration dates can have on states' rankings. The chart depicts the average scale scores in reading from the grade 4 1998 National NAEP. Three months could change the average scale score of a state by 16 points. The arrows are drawn to show that 16 points on this assessment is the difference between the state ranked 5th (Massachusetts) and the state ranked 31st (Arkansas).

SOURCE: Adapted from Donahue et al. (1999).

students from the second state. Similarly, if students who are studying identical content, using the same materials, and following the same sequence of instruction take the same test at different times of the year, students who take the test later in the school term will have an advantage on any test items that measure material covered after students in the first state take the test.

Test Security

The comparability of scores from a test hinges on maintaining comparable levels of test security from one jurisdiction to another. Tight security ensures that students and teachers do not have access to test items before they are administered and that preparation for the test is not focused on specific items. If security is less stringently maintained in one state than in another, scores in the first state may be biased upwards.

Consider what could happen if state A administers a test in October, but state B does not administer it until April. Students and teachers in state B may have the advantage of knowing what is on the test before it is administered and can better prepare for the test.

Additionally, state practices and laws related to test security and the release of test items contained in state tests vary a great deal (see Figure 2-4). Some states release 100 percent of their tests' content every year, others release smaller percentages, and others none at all. But if even one

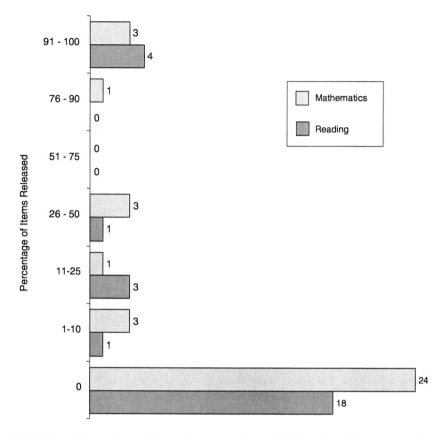

FIGURE 2-4 Items released from 4th-grade reading and 8th-grade mathematics tests in 1997-1998; number of states. NOTE: States are listed more than once when they administered multiple reading or mathematics components and released different percentages of each component. SOURCE: Adapted from Olson et al. (in press).

state releases the items contained in a test, then the items must be changed every year so that breaches in test security and differential examinee exposure to the national test items do not differentially affect student performance.

Breaches in item security can arise not only from state practices related to the release of state test materials. Test security can also be compromised during item development and test production, in test delivery, in test return, and in test disposal. In addition, students may remember particular items and discuss them with other students and teachers. School-based test administrators may remember particular items and incorporate them, or nearly identical items, in their instruction. This problem of inappropriate coaching, or teaching to the test, is especially apparent if the stakes associated with test performance are high.

To circumvent these problems, most commercial testing programs create several equivalent forms of the same test. The equivalent forms may be used on specified test dates or in different jurisdictions. However, creating equivalent versions of the same test is a complex and costly endeavor, and test publishers do not develop unlimited numbers of equivalent forms of the same test. Consequently, varying dates of test administration pose a security risk.

Stakes

Differences in the consequences or "stakes" attached to scores can also threaten comparability of scores earned on the same free-standing test. The stakes associated with test results will affect student test scores by affecting teacher and student perceptions about the importance of the test, the level of student and teacher preparation for the test, and student motivation during the test (see e.g., Kiplinger and Linn, 1996; O'Neil et al., 1992; Wolf et al., 1995; Frederiksen, 1984).

The specific changes in student and teacher behavior spurred by high stakes will determine whether differences in stakes undermine the ability of a free-standing test to provide a common measure of student performance. For example, suppose that state A imposes serious consequences for scores on a specific national test, while state B does not. This difference in stakes could raise scores in state A, relative to those in state B, in two ways. Students and teachers in state A might simply work harder to learn the material the test is designed to represent—the domain. In that case, higher scores in state A would be appropriate, and the common measure would not be undermined. However, teachers in state A might find ways to take shortcuts, tailoring their instruction closely to the content of the test. In that case, gains in scores would be misleadingly large and would not generalize to other tests designed to measure the same domain. In other words, teachers might teach to the test in inappropriate ways that inflate test scores, thus undermining the common measure (see, e.g., Koretz et al., 1996a; Koretz et al., 1996b).

States administer tests for a variety of purposes: student diagnosis, curriculum planning, program evaluation, instructional improvement, promotion/retention decisions, graduation certification, diploma endorsement, and teacher accountability, to name a few. Some of these purposes, such as promotion/retention, graduation certification, diploma endorsement, and accountability, are high stakes for individuals or schools. Others, such as student diagnosis, curriculum planning, program evaluation, and instructional improvement are not.

ABRIDGMENT OF TEST CONTENT FOR EMBEDDING

In the previous section we outlined a variety of conditions that must be met to obtain a common measure and outlined how policies and practices of state testing programs make such conditions difficult to achieve, even when embedding is not involved. Embedding, however, often makes it more difficult to meet these conditions and raises a number of additional issues as well.

Reliability

As long as the items in a test are reasonably similar to each other in terms of the constructs they measure, the reliability of scores will generally increase with the number of items in the test. Thus, when items are reasonably similar, the scores from a longer test will be more stable than those from a shorter test. The effect of chance differences among items, as well as the effect of a single item on the total score, is reduced as the total number of items increases. Embedding an abridged national test in a state test or abridging the state test and giving it with the national test would provide efficiency, compared with administration of the entire state and national tests, but it produces that efficiency by using fewer items. Hence, the scores earned on the abridged test would not be as reliable as scores earned on the unabridged national test. The short length of the abridged test will also increase the likelihood of misleading differences among jurisdictions. Test reliability is a necessary condition for valid inferences from scores.

Content Representation

No set of embedded items, nor any complete test, can possibly tap all of the concepts and processes included in subject areas as complex and heterogeneous as 4th-grade reading and 8th-grade mathematics in the limited time that is usually available for testing. Any collection of items will tap only a limited sample of the skills and knowledge that make up the domain. The items in a national test represent one sample of the domain, and the material selected for embedding represents only a sample of the national test. The smaller the number of items used in embedding, the less likely it is that the embedded material will provide a representative sample of the content and skills that are reflected in the national test in its entirety. How well the national test represents the domain, and how well the embedded material represents the national test, can be affected by both design and chance.

The potentially large effect of differences in sampling from a subject area are illustrated by data from the Iowa Tests of Basic Skills (ITBS) for the state of Iowa (see Figure 2-5). Between 1955 and 1977 the mathematics section of the ITBS consisted of math concepts and math problem-solving tests but did not include a separate math computation test. In 1978 a math computation test was added to the test battery, but the results from this test were not included in the total math score reported in the annual trend data. The trend data from Iowa for 1978-1998 for grade 8 illustrate clearly how quite different inferences might be made about overall trends in math achievement in Iowa depending on whether or not math computation is included in the total math score. Without computation included, it appears that math achievement in Iowa increased steadily from 1978 to the early 1990s and has remained relatively stable since. However, when computation is included in the total math score, overall achievement in 8th-grade mathematics appears to have gone steadily down from its 20-year peak in performance in 1991. Similar differences would be expected in the math performance of individuals, individual school districts, or states depending on whether computation is a major focus of the math curriculum and on how much computation is included in the math test being used to measure performance.

Abridgment of the national test can affect scores even in the absence of systematic decisions to exclude or deemphasize certain content. Even sets of items that are selected at random will differ from each other. Students with similar overall proficiency will often do better on some items than on others. This variation, called "student by task interaction," is the most fundamental source of overall reliability of scores (Gulliksen, 1950; Shavelson et al., 1993; Dunbar et al., 1991; Koretz et al., 1994). Therefore, particularly when the embedded material is short, some students may score considerably differently depending on which sample of items is embedded.

Abridgment could affect not only the scores of individual students, but also the score means of states or districts. As embedded material is

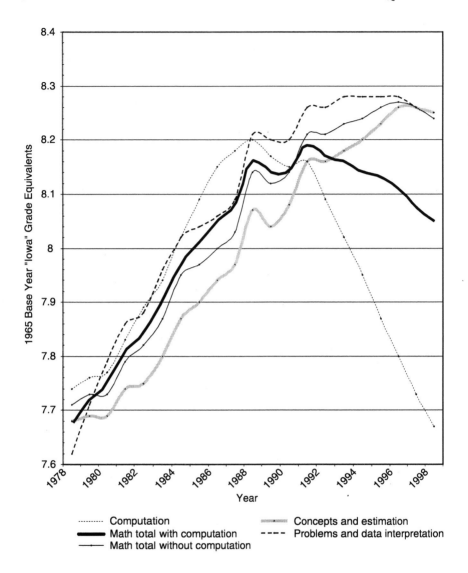

FIGURE 2-5 Iowa trends in achievement in mathematics: 1978-1998, grade 8.
SOURCE: Adapted from Iowa Testing Programs (1999).

abridged, the remaining sample of material may match the curricula in some states better than in others.

PLACEMENT OF EMBEDDED TEST ITEMS

For embedding to be a useful technique for providing a common measure of individual performance in 4th-grade reading and 8th-grade mathematics, there must be an appropriate state test of those subjects into which the national test can be embedded, and conditions must be such that the embedded items can and will be administered under standardized conditions. The diversity of state testing programs and practices which characterizes the American system of education creates an environment in which either or both of these conditions often cannot be met.

Grades and Subjects Tested

Differing state decisions about the purposes for testing lead to differing decisions about what subjects should be tested, who should be tested, and at what point in a student's education testing should occur. For example, some states test students' reading performance in 3rd grade, others in 4th grade. Some states treat reading as a distinct content area and measure it with tests designed to tap the content and skills associated only with reading; others treat reading as one component of a larger subject area, such as language arts, or measure it along with a seemingly unrelated subject such as mathematics.

In the 1997-1998 school year, 41 states tested students in 4th-grade reading, 8th-grade mathematics, or both: 27 states assessed students in reading in 4th grade, and 39 states assessed students in mathematics in 8th grade.[4] Only 25 states tested both 4th-grade reading and 8th-grade mathematics, leaving a significant number of states without tests into which items for those subjects could be embedded (see Table 2-3). It could be possible for states that do not administer reading or mathematics tests in grades 4 and 8, respectively, to embed reading or mathematics items in tests of other subjects, but context effects (see below) could be quite large.

---

[4]Iowa and Nevada do not administer state-mandated assessments; data for the District of Columbia was not available when this report was completed.

TABLE 2-3 Number of States with 4th-Grade Reading, 8th-Grade
Mathematics Assessments, or Both

Types of Testing Programs	Number of States
States with one or more separately scored 4th-grade reading components	27
States with one or more separately scored 8th-grade mathematics components	39
States with both separately scored 4th-grade reading and 8th-grade mathematics components	25

SOURCE: Adapted form Olson et al. (in press).

Context Effects

A context effect occurrs when a change in the test or item setting affects student performance. Context effects are gauged in terms of changes in overall test performance (such as the average test score) or item performance (such as item difficulty). These effects are important because they mean that an item or test is being presented in a way that could make it more difficult for one group of students than another, so that differences in student performance are due not to differences in achievement but to differences in testing conditions. With embedding, it is possible that the changes in the context in which the national items are administered will affect student performance. Such context effects can lead to score inaccuracies and misinterpretations.

An extensive body of research examines the effects of changes in context on student performance.[5] Context effects vary markedly in size, sometimes in respect to differences in tests, but in other cases for unknown reasons. So the research provides a warning that context effects can be large, but it does not provide a clear basis for estimating them in any particular case.

Following are some of the many characteristics on which tests can differ:

---

[5]Interested readers are referred to the review by Leary and Dorans (1985) and the conceptual framework provided by Brennan (1992).

- wording of instructions for items of the same type;
- page design with respect to font and font size, spacing of items, use of illustrative art, use of color, graphics, position of passages relative to related questions, and page navigation aids;
- use of themes (e.g., a carnival as a setting for mathematics items);
- integration of content areas (e.g., reading and language, mathematics computation and problem solving);
- display of answer choices in a vertical string versus a horizontal string;
- convention for ordering numerical answer choices for mathematics items (from smallest to largest or randomly) or ordering of punctuation marks as answer choices for language mechanics items;
- characteristics of manipulatives used with mathematics items (e.g., rulers, protractors);
- degree to which multiple-choice and constructed-response items are integrated during test administration;
- how answer documents are structured for multiple-choice items and constructed-response items;
- number of answer choices; and
- use of "none of the above" as an answer choice.

There are also issues of balance and proportion that occur when items from different tests are integrated, such as: equitable proportions of items that have the keyed (correct) response in each answer choice position and balance in the gender and ethnic characters in items and passages.

In general, as tests become longer, student fatigue becomes more of a factor. An item will tend to be more difficult if it is embedded at the end of a long test than if it is placed at the end of a short test. Similarly, student fatigue tends to be greater at the end of a difficult test— particularly one that involves a lot of reading and constructed responses— than at the end of an easy test. This "difficulty context" can affect the difficulty of embedded items.

An important part of test standardization can be the amount of time that students are given to respond. When tests are lengthened or shortened, or items are moved from one test context to another, it is common to use rules of thumb related to average time-per-item to attempt to maintain comparable standardization conditions. However, such rules do not take into account the fact that some items can take more time than others. They also do not take into account the effects of the surrounding context in terms of test length and test difficulty on the time a student may need for an embedded item.

Tests also vary in terms of their representation of different types of content, and this variance can produce a context effect for embedded items. For example, items related to a poetry passage, or to the Civil War, or to the Pythagorean theorem might be easier if they are embedded in another test with more of that same type of item than if they are embedded in a test with no similar items. The content of individual items can also interact. In constructing tests, careful review takes place so that the information in one item does not give away the correct answer to another item. When items from two tests are integrated, that same review would have to occur.

Constructed-response (open-ended) items bear special mention. The instructions and expectations (in terms of length, detail, conformity to writing conventions, etc.) for constructed responses can vary substantially among tests. Also, many students are more likely to decline to answer a constructed-response item than a multiple-choice item, and the likelihood of responding is affected by the position of the item (Jakwerth et al., 1999). All these factors make constructed-response items particularly susceptible to context effects.

The possibility of context effects can be reduced by prudent, controlled test construction procedures such as: (1) keeping blocks of items intact and maintaining consistent directions and test administration; (2) maintaining the relative position of an item (or block of items) during a testing session; (3) maintaining consistent test length and test difficulty; and (4) making no changes to individual items. Nonetheless, even with careful attempts to follow these suggested test construction procedures, there can be no assurance that context effects have been completely avoided.

SPECIAL ISSUES PERTAINING TO NAEP AND TIMSS

Some embedding plans have the goal of reporting state or district achievement results in terms of the proficiency scales used by the National Assessment of Educational Progress (NAEP), a congressionally mandated achievement survey that first collected data 30 years ago.

Currently, NAEP assesses the achievement of 4th-, 8th-, and 12th-grade students in the nation's schools. Assessments occur every 2 years (in even years), during a 3-month period in the winter. The subject areas vary from one assessment year to the next. For example, in 1996 students were assessed in mathematics and science; in 1998 they were assessed in reading, writing, and civics.

The choice of the NAEP scale for national comparisons may stem from its recent use in comparing states. Originally, NAEP was prohibited from reporting results at the state, district, school, or individual level (Beaton and Zwick, 1992), but legislation passed in 1988 allowed NAEP to report results for individual states that wished to participate. The first such assessment, considered a "trial," was conducted in 1990. The most recent NAEP state assessment included 43 states and jurisdictions. Whereas the national NAEP is administered by a central contractor, the state NAEP assessments are administered by personnel selected by state officials. (See Hartka and McLaughlin (1994) for a discussion of NAEP administration practices and effects.)

NAEP results for the nation and for groups are reported on a numerical scale of achievement that ranges from 0 to 500. The scale supports such statements as, "The average math proficiency of 8th graders has increased since the previous assessment," and "35 percent of state A's students are achieving above the national average." To facilitate interpreting the results in terms of standards of proficiency, panels of experts assembled by the National Assessment Governing Board (the governing body for NAEP) established three points along the scale that represent minimum levels that were judged to represent basic, proficient, and advanced achievement in the subject area. The standards support the use of such phrases as "40 percent of 4th-grade students scored at or above the basic level on this assessment." Note that the three standards divide the scale into four segments, which are often called below basic, basic, proficient, and advanced. These descriptions lead quite naturally to the belief that the NAEP results are obtained by first computing scores for individual students and then aggregating these scores, but this is not the case. The goal of NAEP, as presently designed, is not to provide scores for individual students, but to estimate distributions of results for groups, such as students in the western part of the United States, African-American students, or students whose parents attended college. NAEP's survey design, which allows the most efficient estimation of these group results, differs from the design that would have been chosen had the goal been to optimize the quality of individual scores.

Some special properties of the NAEP design have a bearing on the possibility of embedding part of NAEP in another assessment. The important differences between NAEP and conventional tests are summarized here (see also National Research Council, 1999a; National Research Council, 1999b). Technical details can be found in sets of papers on NAEP that appeared in special issues of the *Journal of Educational Statistics* (1992) and the *Journal of Educational Measurement* (1992).

First, NAEP is a survey, not an individual achievement test. Its design does not allow the computation of reliable individual scores; instead, it is designed to optimize the quality of achievement results for *groups* (e.g., "4th-grade girls whose mothers have at least a college education"). Second, students who participate in NAEP do not receive identical sets of test questions. For example, in the main portion of the 1996 assessment, more than 60 different booklets were administered at each grade. Third, because of NAEP's complex design, the proper statistical analysis of NAEP data requires an understanding of weighting and variance estimation procedures for complex samples and of data imputation methods. Ignoring the special features of the data will, in general, lead to misleading conclusions.

NAEP keeps testing burden to a minimum by testing only a small sample of students, and by testing each student on only a small sample of the items in the assessment. Each tested student receives two or three of the eight or more booklets of items that together constitute the assessment in a given subject area. The booklets are not alternate test forms that would provide similar scores for individual students. The content, difficulty, and number of items vary across the booklets, and no single booklet is representative of the content domain. This approach to the distribution of items to test takers, called matrix sampling, allows coverage of a broad range of content without imposing a heavy testing burden on individual students.

Within the context of NAEP, these features do not present a major obstacle since the proficiency results for students are examined only after they are pooled in estimating group results. As noted above, the data must be aggregated using elaborate statistical methods to obtain group estimates of proficiency for the nation and for specified groups. However, the nonequivalence of the various NAEP booklets within an assessment would be problematic if scores were to be obtained and compared for individual students.

One way to obtain individual student scores on NAEP would be to construct a test of reasonable length in each subject area that covered the same material as NAEP, albeit not as thoroughly. The proposed Voluntary National Tests (VNT) is such an effort. The VNT is being planned as a conventional test that will yield individual student scores on a scale as similar as possible to the NAEP scale. The VNT is intended to provide a common metric for reporting achievement results for all test takers. Many of the proponents of embedding hope to achieve this same goal without imposing an additional testing burden on individuals, districts, or states.

In many respects, the design of TIMSS mirrors that of NAEP (see Martin and Kelly (1996) for a detailed description of TIMSS). TIMSS, like NAEP, used matrix sampling of items to increase breadth of content coverage while limiting testing time. The assessment consisted of several different booklets, which were randomly distributed to students. TIMSS, like NAEP, was designed for efficient estimation of the proficiency of groups, rather than individuals; as in NAEP, individual scores are not reported for students.

3

Three Designs for Embedding

The issues raised in the preceding chapter lay the groundwork for evaluating embedding as a method of providing national scores for individual students. In this chapter the discussion focuses on three specific procedures for embedding, illustrated by three scenarios. The scenarios exemplify the general approaches that are most likely to be used at present to obtain national scores for individuals. Variants of these approaches might have somewhat different strengths and weaknesses, but the basic issues that arise in evaluating these three scenarios will apply.

The basis for comparison for evaluating the three embedding scenarios is the administration of both the state and national assessments in their entirety—two free-standing tests—discussed in Chapter 2. As is noted there, if the national test is administered following the procedures that were used when the test was standardized, and if the inferences drawn from the national test are appropriate—two major conditions—the approach can provide comparable national scores for individual students in different states.

Embedding creates at least one and often two changes, compared with two free-standing tests. First, one test is abridged. Second, to varying degrees, embedding generally changes the conditions of administration from those that would exist if the two tests were administered in their entirety and independently.

EMBEDDING WITHOUT ABRIDGMENT OF THE NATIONAL TEST: THE DOUBLE-DUTY SCENARIO

Administering a complete state test along with an entire national test—the two free-standing tests approach—involves some redundancy and wasted resources. The double-duty scenario is an effort to increase efficiency and reduce testing time by having some items from the national test serve a double duty, contributing to both national and state scores without requiring the student to respond to duplicative items that measure the same construct, once as part of the national test and again as part of a state test. A number of states are currently using this approach in their state testing programs. The committee did not deliberate at length about the change in burden to states that implement the double-duty approach. However, we note that more than 20 states have already adopted this approach of their own accord, which suggests that they find it on balance worthwhile.

Design and Features

Before implementing this approach, state testing experts develop specifications for a state test (see Chapter 2). They compare these specifications with commercially published standardized achievement tests that produce individual student scores. Some of the items in these national tests match the state's test specifications closely; others do not. To gain the most efficiency, the state experts choose the national test that most closely matches their state's test specifications. They then identify the specific items in the national test that measure state standards and custom-develop items to measure any state specifications not sampled by the national test. Some states might use a large part of the national test for generating state scores; others might use very little of it.

Administration

The national test is administered in its entirety under its prescribed standardized conditions. State test items are not physically embedded in the national test, but they are administered close in time under whatever conditions the state determines to be appropriate. This administration procedure protects the national test from context effects.

Scoring and Analysis

As with two free-standing tests, in this scenario a student receives two sets of scores: a national score and a state score. The two scores are not independent because student responses to some national test items count in the state score as well as in the national score.

The national score reflects the entire national test; it is the same as would be obtained if the national test were administered with no connection to the state custom-developed items because the national test is not modified and is administered under its standardized conditions. Thus, the psychometric quality of those scores (reliability, validity) are those the national test normally provides.

The state score reflects a student's responses to two sets of items: all of the custom-developed state items and the subset of items from the national test that pertain to the state's test specifications (see Figure 3-1). This subset might be most or little of the national test, depending on a judgment about the extent of the match between the state's curriculum and the content of the national test.

For the state items, scoring procedures are developed and used as deemed appropriate by the state's educators. It is necessary to keep track of which items from the national test "count" in calculating the state score; it is these items that do double duty. The state education agency develops scores that meet its needs, such as a state-specific scale score or performance level system or state norms. The state items provide no scores referenced to national norms or performance levels.

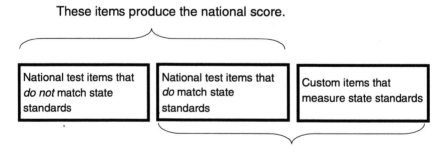

FIGURE 3-1 The double-duty scenario.

Evaluation

The double-duty approach differs in a few key respects from the model of embedding that was the focus of Congress' charge to the committee. These differences are central to the evaluation of this approach to embedding.

Advantages

The gains in efficiency from this approach stem from eliminating the redundancy that occurs when students are asked to respond twice, on two different tests, to the same or similar items. The double-duty approach entails no abridgment of the national test. Accordingly, the troublesome issues noted in Chapter 2 that result from abridgment do not apply to the national test in the double-duty scenario.

The national test is administered in all jurisdictions following the procedures prescribed by the test publisher. Assuming that the state items are administered close in time to the national test, rather than at the same time, they are unlikely to change responses to the national test appreciably. For these reasons, the double-duty approach provides national scores for individual students that are essentially the same in quality as those that would be obtained in the absence of embedding.

Since most commercially available large-scale assessments provide different norms for different testing dates, the testing date for the national test is flexible if one of these tests is selected as the national test. The national test can be administered at a time that is convenient and appropriate for the administration of the state test (see Chapter 2).

Disadvantages

The success of the double-duty approach hinges on having an agreed-on national test that provides individual student scores. Currently, there is no such single national test. Thus, comparability of national scores is limited to the states that administer the same national test. Furthermore, this approach cannot be used with national tests that are matrix sampled in a manner that precludes providing individual scores—for example, NAEP.

The degree to which the double-duty approach provides efficiency gains while providing much the same information as would be obtained by administering two free-standing tests in their entirety depends on there being substantial overlap in content between the national test and state curricula. The weaker the match between the content of the national test and state standards, the less the benefit of efficiency through double-duty items.

The two scores, state and national, may differ due to measurement error or a poor match between a state's curriculum and the national test. Such differences in scores can be confusing to students, parents, school administrators, and the public if they are not clearly explained.

In the double-duty scenario, some of the items that contribute to the state score are administered as part of the national test, rather than with the customized items developed by the state for its own purposes. To the extent that the administration of the national test differs from that of the state's custom items, students' performance on these items may be different than it would have been if they had been administered with the state's custom items because of factors discussed in the preceding chapter. For example, context effects could change students' performance on these items. The committee did not deliberate on the likely effects of these factors on state scores under the double-duty scenario.

Finally, in the current environment of varying but often intense accountability pressures, the national information obtained through the double-duty scenario will sometimes be suspect. That is, if teachers and students feel pressure to raise state scores and if part of the national test contributes to state scores, there may be incentives to engage in the types of inappropriate teaching to the test that can inflate scores. This effect could make the national scores and comparisons among jurisdictions misleading in some instances.

EMBEDDING REPRESENTATIVE MATERIAL: THE NAEP-BLOCKS SCENARIO

More pertinent to Congress' question than the double-duty scenario, but less commonly observed in practice, are embedding approaches in which a national test is abridged and the extract from the national test is embedded in a full state test. One variant of this approach is the NAEP-blocks scenario, in which a portion of NAEP is embedded in a state assessment.

Design and Features

Three blocks taken from either the 8th-grade NAEP mathematics assessment or the 4th-grade reading assessment are administered contem-

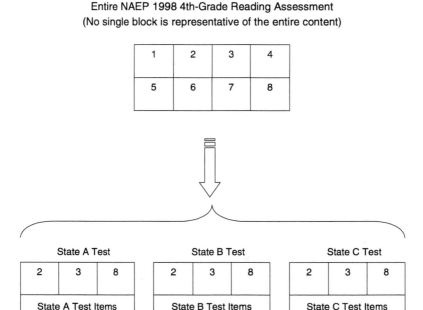

Entire NAEP 1998 4th-Grade Reading Assessment
(No single block is representative of the entire content)

FIGURE 3-2 The NAEP-blocks scenario. States insert the same three unaltered NAEP blocks into their tests. The state tests may vary in content, format, length, level of difficulty, usage, stakes, administration practices, and policies for the inclusion and accommodation of students with disabilities or limited English proficiency.

poraneously and intact, with separate timing, as a part of the state assessment.[1] All students take the embedded blocks along with the state assessment; see Figure 3-2.

The NAEP blocks can be either physically or conceptually embedded in the state assessment. If they are physically embedded, they would presumably be administered first in order to minimize context effects. If

---

[1]NAEP normally administers its assessments of a subject matter in several short segments, called blocks, that are not designed to be parallel in content. In 1996 the entire NAEP 8th-grade mathematics assessment contained 13 blocks of items, each 15 or 20 minutes in length. The complete 1998 NAEP 4th-grade reading assessment contained 8 blocks of items, each of which was 25 minutes in length. The test booklets that are administered to individual students have different combinations of these blocks, and each test booklet includes only a fraction of the total assessment.

the NAEP blocks are not physically embedded, they would be administered within a short time of the state test.

The NAEP-blocks scenario illustrates one way of choosing between local control and consistency of national testing. In this scenario, local control is limited, and standardization of national testing among states is substantial. States cannot pick items individually; all items within the chosen blocks are used, and no items from other blocks are added.

Administration

In this scenario the state assessment is administered in its entirety. The administration of the embedded blocks mimics the administration of NAEP as much as possible in order to minimize distortions arising from administrative differences. For example, the date of administration would fall near the midpoint of NAEP's range of testing dates. Similarly, electronic calculators would be provided for the items in the selected NAEP mathematics blocks that require their use. NAEP guidelines for inclusion and use of accommodations would be followed. Students who are unfamiliar with the format of NAEP questions would be provided with a pretest orientation.

Administration of three embedded blocks requires approximately 45-75 minutes of testing time. Embedding more blocks would increase the accuracy of student scores and would improve the representation of NAEP content, but at the cost of creating an additional testing burden.

Scoring and Analysis

Students receive two scores: scores that are normally provided from the state assessment and a designation of their NAEP performance level and possibly their NAEP proficiency score, along with an indication of the associated margin of error.

The state score is based on either the state test alone or the state test in conjunction with any NAEP items the state considers appropriate. The national score is based on the NAEP items alone. In theory, the NAEP items could be linked to state items to provide a more reliable estimate of student performance, but as noted in *Uncommon Measures* (National Research Council, 1999c), this approach faces major obstacles and is generally not practical.

The state assessment is analyzed and scored separately, using the same procedures that are normally used for that state assessment. The

NAEP items are scored separately.[2]   The item responses are used, with the NAEP item information, to estimate a NAEP proficiency score for each student, as well as the performance level of the student. The quality of the link between student performance on the embedded items and the NAEP scale will depend on the length of the embedded segment and on how well it represents the full national assessment. A more elaborate version of this plan could be used to link the state assessment with the NAEP scale. It would involve a very substantial investment in a unique statistical analysis, and it would be subject to the problems that exist for any link, if the NAEP assessment does not match the state assessment.

Evaluation

As noted, this scenario was chosen to illustrate a relatively high level of standardization across states and a relatively low level of local control.

Advantages

The requirement that states use the same fixed set of NAEP blocks would provide a consistent basis for comparisons among states. In addition, this scenario makes the embedded material more nearly representative of the NAEP assessment than it would be if items were chosen freely by states. In general, the increase in standardization—of content and administration—would increase the comparability of scores across states.

Disadvantages

In practice, the NAEP-blocks scenario faces substantial obstacles. Although states use a fixed set of NAEP blocks, the content of the embedded material would not be fully representative of NAEP. Individual NAEP blocks are not constructed to represent the entirety of the assessment, and even a set of three blocks is likely to provide an unbalanced or less than complete representation of the NAEP assessment. This lack of representativeness would likely be exacerbated if states are restricted to using publicly released NAEP blocks, which is likely, because allowing

---

[2]NAEP blocks include open-ended responses that must be scored by trained raters— placing a burden on the state to train the raters using the NAEP procedures or to hire the NAEP scoring subcontractor to score them.

widespread use of unreleased NAEP blocks would jeopardize NAEP's security and threaten the integrity of NAEP results.

Even if the content of the embedded blocks were fully representative of NAEP, it would be difficult to obtain scores comparable to the performance estimates provided by NAEP. NAEP uses an elaborate statistical process called "conditioning" (see, e.g., Beaton and Gonzales, 1995) to adjust for the fact that each student takes a different, small part of the full assessment. This process creates some intermediate computed quantities called "plausible values" for each student, based on both cognitive information (performance on test items) and noncognitive information (characteristics of students). When aggregated with similar values from other test takers, these quantities provide good estimates of the distribution of student performance on the NAEP scale. However, the plausible values are not scores. A different method of scoring, based only on a student's performance on the test items, would be needed for generating individual student scores. One consequence of the changed method of scoring is that the distribution of the resulting scores from embedding would differ from the reported NAEP distributions.

In addition, administration conditions, time of testing, and criteria for excluding students from participation because of disabilities or limited proficiency in English may not be the same for the NAEP items administered with the state test as for the same items administered as part of NAEP. Consequently, states might be required to administer their state assessments at a time that is more appropriate for the embedded test than for their own tests and to follow NAEP guidelines for inclusion and accommodation of students with disabilities and limited proficiency in English.

Motivational differences are another threat to the comparability of scores. Students face no consequences for their performance on NAEP as it is currently administered. In the current climate of accountability, however, they (or their teachers, or both) often face serious consequences for their scores on state tests. This difference could result in scores on the embedded material that are higher than those on NAEP itself for students with identical levels of proficiency.

Context effects could also make scores noncomparable (see Chapter 2). One could minimize these effects by administering the NAEP items separately or at the beginning of the state test. However, such tactics might not suffice to eliminate context effects entirely. For example, if NAEP items were presented first, performance might be affected by the overall directions given at the outset of the test or by the prospect of a lengthier testing period than that of NAEP. Similarly, even with efforts to standardize administration, some unintended differences in administration might remain, and these could undermine the comparability of scores (see Hartka and McLaughlin, 1994).

Because the precision of scores is in part a function of the length of a test, embedding poses a tradeoff between accuracy and burden. The NAEP-blocks scenario would add 45-75 minutes of testing time per subject, yet it would provide very imprecise estimates of the performance of individual students—too imprecise for many purposes. If estimated scores are used to provide a performance-level classification, the classification would be prone to error.

A study using similar methodology was conducted by McLaughlin (1998), who reported that a 95 percent confidence interval spanned a range of 70 points for an estimated individual NAEP score on 8th-grade mathematics. Given this confidence interval width, approximately 14 percent of the students could be expected to be classified in a level below their true achievement level, and about 16 percent in a higher level, with about 70 percent assigned to the correct performance level.

Finally, embedding NAEP blocks could have undesirable consequences for NAEP. As noted, if secure blocks are used for embedding, the additional exposure of these blocks could undermine the comparability of NAEP scores. For example, if some teachers tailor instruction directly to secure NAEP items because they expect them to appear on state tests, the result could be distortions of comparisons that are based on NAEP scores. NAEP trends might appear more favorable than they really are, and some comparisons among states could be biased. Depending on the degree of similarity between released and secure blocks, embedding released blocks could also threaten NAEP scores, although probably less so.

EMBEDDING UNREPRESENTATIVE MATERIAL: THE ITEM-BANK SCENARIO

A counterpoint to the NAEP-blocks scenario is the item-bank scenario, which entails a great degree of local discretion and accordingly less standardization.

Design and Features

In the item-bank scenario, a set of test items is made available to a state testing agency. These items may come from a well-established national or international assessment program, such as NAEP or the Third International Mathematics and Science Study (TIMSS), or any other respected source, such as an interstate item development and testing consortium or a commercial test publisher's existing item banks, or they can be created specifically for use in the item bank. The items are calibrated—that is, their difficulty is estimated—with information from a national calibration study. In some respects, the item bank is like a very long national test. State testing agencies choose items from the bank, individually or in sets, and include the selected items in their state tests.

Although item banks can be used in various ways, in this scenario it is assumed that states choose items on the basis of a match with their curricula or other considerations, with no consideration given to maintaining comparability across states in the items selected. States can also choose varying numbers of items to embed.

Selected items are physically embedded in the state assessment and can be either freely interspersed or inserted as one or more discrete blocks. Timing and administrative conditions are determined by the individual state testing programs.

Administration

The selected national items are interspersed in the state test and the state test, including the embedded items, is administered as a single unit; see Figure 3-3.

Scoring and Analysis

Students receive two scores, a state score and a national score. The state score could be based either on the state items alone or on a combination of the state items and some or all of the items chosen from the item bank. Similarly, the national score could be based either on the national items alone or by linking them with some of the state items. In these respects, the item-bank approach is similar to the NAEP-blocks approach.

This design can theoretically produce individual national scores on any national test, including assessments such as NAEP or TIMSS. However, the content of NAEP and TIMSS is broader than that which would normally be covered by an individually administered assessment, let alone a small number of embedded items. Therefore, NAEP and TIMSS are unlikely candidates for the national score that this scenario could produce.

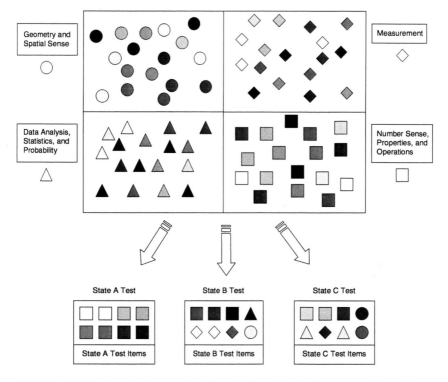

FIGURE 3-3 The item-bank scenario. States independently choose items from a hypothetical mathematics item bank. In practice, there would be far more items than are represented here. The shading of the symbols indicates that the items may vary along important dimensions other than content, such as difficulty and format. There are variations among subsets of the item bank that might be embedded into different state tests.

Evaluation

As noted, the item-bank scenario represents the greatest amount of local control and the least amount of standardization across jurisdictions. It is also the only scenario that involves embedding items that are not common to all states.

Advantages

For certain purposes, the item-bank scenario has advantages relative to the NAEP-blocks scenario. For example, embedding items from an item pool responds to the desire to maintain state standards by placing all control for selecting items, administering a test, and constructing scores with the state testing agency.

For some purposes it is a convenient method for providing localities and states with well-constructed, field-tested items. In some situations it is also very efficient; it allows states to use items relevant to their purposes without expending state resources or testing time on items of little interest to them.

Disadvantages

The item-bank scenario is very poorly suited for the purpose of providing comparable national scores for individual students. For this purpose, it shares the problems noted for the NAEP-blocks design and faces numerous others, as well.

The element of choice entailed by the item-bank scenario undermines the comparability of ostensibly national scores. The subsets of items chosen by states would not necessarily be representative of the item pool itself and would not have to be similar across states. States could choose items on which their students are likely to do particularly well, given their curricula, and avoid those on which their students are likely to do poorly. Indeed, simply attempting to align the selected items with curricula would likely bias scores upward, relative to those that would be obtained if the entire item bank, or a representative sample from it, were used.

In other words, the process of choice would undermine the calibration of items provided by the national calibration sample. By allowing states to choose items freely, the system also allows them to reallocate instructional effort away from excluded items and toward included ones. Such an effect will make included items seem easier, and it would similarly make excluded ones seem harder.

The item-bank scenario also raises problems of item security, some of which are more serious than those raised by the NAEP-blocks scenario. For example, suppose that state A uses certain items in March testing, while state B uses some of the same items in late April. Information on the items used in state A might be obtained by teachers or students in state B, allowing inappropriate coaching that would inflate scores. If the embedded items come from a secure source, such as nonreleased NAEP blocks or commercial test publishers' item banks, embedding them repeatedly in state assessments undermines their security. If the national item pool is developed from publicly released items, such as released NAEP blocks, issues related to familiarity with the items or inappropriate teaching to the test may undermine the comparability of the scores.

Because the item-bank scenario does not impose uniformity of scheduling or administration, differences in these factors could also undermine the comparability of scores across states. States might differ, for example, in terms of the dates chosen for testing, the placement of embedded items, the degree of time pressure imposed in testing, the inclusion of low-achieving groups, the use of accommodations, or many other aspects of administration. As noted in Chapter 2, each of these factors has the potential to affect scores substantially, thus undermining comparability.

The item-bank scenario poses a considerable state burden for data analysis, and the possibility of untimely reporting of scores. Obtaining a common measure will involve time-consuming, burdensome data analysis of empirical results. Data must either come from pretesting the entire assessment in another jurisdiction or from data from the current assessment. Pretesting must be done a year in advance, to avoid the time-of-year problem (see Chapter 2). Using data from the current assessment means that scores cannot be reported immediately, but must wait several months for the analyses to be completed.

Finally, states would have to deal with the political difficulty of different test scores from the "same" test administration that rank students differently, since two distinct scores are reported.

EVALUATION OF THE SCENARIOS

The three scenarios differ along several dimensions: the representativeness of the embedded material versus added testing burden for students; the amount of standardization in administration versus the degree of local control; and the extent of the burden placed on states.

A major purpose of embedding is to provide two scores, a national and a state score, without significantly adding to the amount of time a student spends taking tests. The standard of comparison, two freestanding tests, creates the largest testing burden. Since all of the embedding scenarios involve abridging one or the other of the two tests, the testing burden is reduced relative to administering two tests in their entirety. The relative gains in efficiency, however, depend largely on the degree of abridgment. There is a tradeoff: the greater the degree of abridgment, the greater the likelihood that the abridgment could lead to lower score accuracy (see Chapter 2).

All three scenarios require some change in the state test or testing program. Such changes may interrupt long-term trend information that is of value to the states. For example, some states have developed elaborate test-based accountability systems that rely on longitudinal analysis of test data, the results of which are used to support high-stakes rewards and sanctions for schools and districts.

Some states construct their examination forms so that the difficulty level of the overall test is similar from year to year. If the items to be embedded have differing overall difficulty levels, one form of the test could become more difficult than another—particularly if the embedded material changes from year to year.

The validity of the state tests may be compromised if embedded items appear in the middle of an examination and represent material the students have not had the opportunity to learn. For many students, this situation could cause additional anxiety, resulting in a lower score. This is a particular problem when the national test is physically embedded in the state test, as is the case with the item-bank and the NAEP-blocks scenarios.

Other issues also arise. For example, if the national test that is selected has norms at only one grade and testing date (e.g., the proposed VNT or NAEP), the state agency must administer that test at the grade and testing date dictated by the national test, even if it is not an optimum time for the state's own test to be administered. If states want different items to appear in the state test in different years, for security or other purposes, the state education agency will have to construct tests that are parallel in content and psychometric characteristics from year to year and to perform appropriate equating analyses. This is a difficult and costly endeavor.

If national items are physically embedded in state tests, the various accommodations that are made available for the state tests would have to be available for the embedded items. Suppose each state makes all of its accommodations available for the national items (which at best may involve considerable work and expense and at worst may not be possible): then the national items will vary from state to state in how they are administered, which violates an essential condition for obtaining a common measure. This result effectively renders the results from the national items noncomparable across states—unless all of the states can be convinced to offer the same accommodations. When the national test is administered separately, differences in accommodation practices among states will not affect national scores, but they will affect the type of information that is available for accommodated students. These students will earn only a partial state score. Partial data decreases the amount and type of achievement information that can be made available to them, their parents, and their teachers.

All of the embedding scenarios make considerable demands on local resources in terms of development, analysis of test items, or both. For example, in the NAEP-blocks scenario, although the National Assessment Governing Board (NAGB) selects and makes available a set of NAEP blocks, together with the procedures for scoring them, states will have to train staff to score the constructed-response items or else contract with the organization that scores NAEP items for NAGB. The demand on state resources is even greater for the item-bank scenario, since much technical work is involved at the item level and a linking study would be required. All three scenarios can also place additional financial burdens on states, especially true if states are asked to bear any of the cost for development of new state tests, data analysis, additional scoring, or printing and distributing new test booklets.

All three scenarios also raise the problem of timelines. Timeliness in reporting scores requires much advanced preparation, and extensive data analysis, which may strain local resources. In the NAEP-blocks and the item-bank scenarios, if local items are to be combined with the national items, the necessary analyses cannot readily be done before giving the assessment. But if the analyses must be done after the assessment has been given, the scores will not be available to students, parents, or teachers in a timely fashion. A student beginning the 9th grade might not benefit from learning that his or her 8th-grade mathematics performance was at a basic level. Students and their teachers want to know how they are doing now, not how they did 6 months ago. In the double-duty scenario, the national score can be provided very quickly, but the local data might be slow in coming, because student scores on the state items cannot be provided before national test results are made available.

Although embedding appears at first to be a practical answer to policy makers' goal of obtaining data on student achievement relative to national standards with little or no added test burden for students and minimum disruption of state testing programs, myriad problems, as illustrated by these three scenarios, make that goal elusive.

4

Common Measures for Purposes
Other Than Individual Scores

Although education policy makers are interested in using embedding to develop comparable measures of individual student performance, many also want to know if embedding can be used to develop a common measure that can be used for other purposes. Those purposes include: reporting aggregated statistics for schools or districts on the scale of NAEP or another well-regarded national test; comparing state performance standards against national performance standards that are considered rigorous; reporting state performance on the NAEP scale in years when state NAEP is not administered or when particular subjects are not included in the NAEP assessment for that year; and auditing yearly gains on state tests. Accordingly, we comment briefly in this chapter on a number of such potential uses of embedding parts of a national test in state tests.

In considering the feasibility of using embedding to develop a common measure of aggregate performance, we use the same definition of a common measure that we use throughout the report: a common measure is a single scale of measurement; scores from tests that are calibrated to such a scale support the same inferences about student performance from one locality to another and from one year to the next.

The requirements for valid score interpretation are no less challenging in this context (aggregated results) than they are in the more familiar individual-differences context. Moreover, the evidence that might support the interpretations and uses of the test scores for individual students does not necessarily support the interpretations and policy uses of aggregated results (Linn, 1993a:5).

Many of the threats to inferences from embedded material stem from systematic differences among jurisdictions (see Chapter 2), which pose obstacles to the use of embedding to provide aggregated national scores for groups (e.g., schools or districts), just as they impede the provision of individual student scores. Below is a very brief discussion about the use of embedding to develop a common measure for aggregates.

PROVIDING NATIONAL SCORES FOR AGGREGATES

States may be interested in obtaining national scores for aggregates, such as schools or districts. These aggregated national scores might be tied to NAEP or to another national test. Currently, the National Assessment Governing Board (NAGB) is considering options for providing district results for some districts that meet particular guidelines for participation. Their plans, which were discussed at the March 4-6, 1999, May 13-15, 1999, and August 5-7, 1999, board meetings, do not rely on either embedding or linking.

How is providing a common measure of district and school performance from embedding NAEP items or blocks in state tests the same as or different from providing a common measure of individual performance that is derived from embedded items? On the positive side, some of the things that affect the scores earned by individual students will average out in the aggregate. For example, students have good days and bad days, depending on their health, mood, amount of sleep, and so on. These factors can cause students' individual scores to fluctuate from day to day. In the aggregate, however, these fluctuations tend to average out and will therefore have less effect on the average test score earned by an entire school, and less yet on the average score obtained for an entire district. When only errors of this sort are involved, the precision of the estimate increases with the size of the group on which it is based.

Similarly, the decrease in the reliability of individual scores that is caused by abridging the content of the national test to facilitate embedding is somewhat mitigated when aggregated scores are calculated. In addition, assessments that do not produce individual student scores can be designed to lessen the effect of abridgment by using a matrix-sampled design. With a design of this sort, individual students are administered abridged and sometimes unrepresentative portions of the test, but aggregated scores will still reflect the entirety of the test. This approach is used in both TIMSS and NAEP and could be used in an embedding design as well, as long as aggregated scores are the purpose of the embedding.

On the negative side, however, many of the potential threats to valid inferences about individual students (discussed in Chapter 2) do not average out and therefore also pose serious threats to aggregated scores. These are factors that differ from one aggregate (e.g., classroom, school, or district) to another, not from one student to the next. For example, as discussed in Chapter 2, a variety of differences in context and administration could bias estimates of national scores for individual students. Students with the same level of mastery of the material should receive similar scores, but if a test is administered to them differently, they might obtain dissimilar scores solely because of those differences in administration. Among these differences in context and administration are decisions about which students are tested or excluded, the types of accommodations offered to students with special needs, and the dates on which tests are administered. These factors do not vary among students within a group, but between groups. For example, two states may set different dates for test administration, but all students within each state will take the test at approximately the same time. When a given factor does not vary within the aggregate—whether it be a school, a district, or an entire state—combining results from students within that group will not average out its effects.

This problem is illustrated by rules for the inclusion of students with disabilities or with limited proficiency in English. State rules for the inclusion of these students in state testing programs vary markedly. The 1998 *Annual Survey of State Student Assessment Programs,* conducted by the Council of Chief State School Officers, indicated ·that most states leave decisions about the exclusion of students with limited English proficiency from state assessments to local committees or to the schools themselves (Olson et al., in press). In some states, such as California and New Mexico, such students account for more than 20 percent of the total, and the lack of comparability of inclusion guidelines could have a significant effect on state test results. The passage of the 1997 amendments to the Individuals with Disabilities Education Act (IDEA) is expected to lead to somewhat greater uniformity in inclusion practices for students with disabilities, but the decision regarding inclusion rests with school officials in most states, and there still may be significant state-to-state differences regarding which students are tested.

The most recent NAEP state-by-state reading results illustrate the effect that different decisions on inclusion may have on exam results. A study conducted by the Educational Testing Service for the National Center for Education Statistics found that an increase in the number of low-achieving students excluded from the assessment could boost the apparent increase in states' reading scores (Mazzeo et al., 1999). A worst-case model found that gains posted by at least two states might have been influenced appreciably by such increases in exclusion. Similarly, differences in the accommodations offered to students with disabilities who are included in the assessment can substantially alter aggregated scores (Halla, 1988; Huesman, 1999; Rudman and Raudenbush, 1996; Whitney and Patience, 1981). In comparing the scores from state testing programs, it is important to note that states do not uniformly include scores earned by disabled and limited-English-proficient students who were allowed accommodations during testing in their aggregated score summary reports (Olson et al., in press).

STATE PERFORMANCE STANDARDS

Although it has never been formally published, Musick's "Setting Education Standards High Enough" is one of the most frequently requested publications produced by the Southern Regional Education Board. In it, Musick (1996:1) succinctly presents the issue of varying state standards:

> If [states] don't talk to each other, the odds are great that 1) many states will set low performance standards for student achievement despite lofty sounding pronouncements about high standards, and 2) the standards for student achievement will be so dramatically different from state to state that they simply won't make sense . . . If what is taught in eighth grade mathematics in one state is much the same as what is taught in eighth grade mathematics in another state, how do we explain that one state has 84 percent of its students meeting its performance standards for student achievement while another state has 13 percent of its students meeting its standard? Do we really believe that this dramatic difference is in what these eighth grade students know about mathematics? Or is it possible that much of the difference is because one state has a low performance standard for student achievement and the other has a higher standard.

Its release in 1996 led policy makers across the country to ask, "Are our state's standards high enough?" To answer policy makers' question—and the related concern that some state standards may be unrealistically high—it has been suggested that what is needed is corroborative data from a national assessment on which standards are rigorous and widely accepted. The reporting metrics of NAEP, TIMSS, and the Organization for Economic Co-operation and Development's Programme for International Student Assessment (PISA) are mentioned as possible rulers against which state policy makers could gauge the relative difficulty of their performance standards.

The desire for this type of information leads to the question of whether strategies to embed items taken from one of these tests can be implemented for this purpose. Embedding has been used in this way in Louisiana. Hill and his associates (Childs and Hill, 1998) embedded released NAEP blocks in a field test of items for the new Louisiana Educational Assessment Program (LEAP) in order to put the LEAP items and the NAEP items on the same proficiency scale. They used the scale to compare the Louisiana performance standards with the NAEP performance standards. The main goal was simply to see if the Louisiana standards were as difficult as the national standards. The result of their study was that the state standards were deemed to be at least as difficult as the NAEP standards.

ESTIMATING STATE NAEP RESULTS IN YEARS THAT STATE NAEP IS NOT ADMINISTERED

States may be interested in obtaining estimates of performance relative to NAEP achievement levels or the NAEP scale for years when the NAEP state assessment is not administered in order to monitor progress and support trends with additional data points. Some policy makers and researchers have expressed an interest in using linking or embedding to obtain these estimates from state testing programs (McLaughlin, 1998; Bock and Zimowski, 1999).

If embedding is to be used for this purpose, the issues that arise are much the same as those that arise in any effort to link a state test to the NAEP scales or interpret the results in terms of NAEP performance standards (see Chapter 2). They are also the same as those issues that arise when trying to provide lower-level aggregated national scores by embedding NAEP items in state tests (see discussion above).

AUDITING THE RESULTS OF DISTRICT AND STATE ASSESSMENTS

Some states (or critics of state programs) are interested in using results from state NAEP or other tests, such as commercially available, norm-referenced tests, to validate gains on state tests. They argue that if gains on a state test are meaningful, they should be at least partly reflected in the states' performance on a well-respected external measure of student performance that tests the same subject area.

Auditing of this sort can be done on a limited scale with no linking or embedding whatsoever. For example, Hambleton et al. (1995) and Koretz and Barron (1998) evaluated gains on Kentucky's state test by comparing trends to those on state NAEP. However, the advantages and disadvantages of embedding national items in state tests to validate gains on state tests remain largely unexplored. It is not clear whether embedding would increase or decrease the accuracy of the inferences from auditing. Moreover, embedding NAEP blocks or material from any commercially available norm-referenced test could have undesirable consequences for the national test that serves as the source of the embedded items, especially if secure NAEP blocks are used for embedding. The additional exposure of these blocks could undermine the comparability of NAEP results, both across jurisdictions and over time. Thus, this use of embedding could necessitate increased development of test items and equating of those new items with existing items

5

Conclusions

The type of embedding that the committee considered to be most central to its charge is including parts of a national assessment in state assessment programs in order to provide individual students with national scores that are (1) comparable with the scores that would have been obtained had the national assessment been administered to them in its entirety and (2) comparable from state to state. The embedded material could be generated from fixed portions of a national assessment or it could comprise test questions chosen by state policy makers. The national scores could be obtained either with or without statistical linkage between the embedded material and the questions in the state assessment.

CONCLUSION 1: Embedding part of a national assessment in state assessments will not provide valid, reliable, and comparable national scores for individual students as long as there are (1) substantial differences in content, format, or administration between the embedded material and the national test that it represents or (2) substantial differences in context or administration between the state and national testing programs that change the ways in which students respond to the embedded items.

National scores that are derived from an embedded national test or test items are likely to be both imprecise and biased, and the direction and extent of bias is likely to vary in important ways—e.g., across population groups and across schools with different curricula. The impediments to deriving valid, reliable, and comparable national scores from embedded items stem from three sources: differences between the state and national tests; differences between the state and national testing programs, such as the procedures used for test administration; and differences between the embedded material and the national test from which it is drawn.

When the state and national tests differ substantially in emphasis (content, format, difficulty, etc.), performance on the embedded material may be appreciably different when it is included with the state test than it is in the national test. That is, performance may be influenced by the different context in which items are presented. As a result, seemingly similar levels of performance are likely to have different meanings.

Inferences about individual performance from embedded test material similarly could be substantially distorted by many differences between the national and state testing program in administration and context, regardless of the characteristics of the two tests and the embedded items. Under the rubric of "administration and context" we include: differences in the time of year at which the test is administered; differences in test context (i.e., the surrounding test material); differences in the broader context (such as differences in motivation stemming from high stakes); differences in assessment accommodations for students with special needs; and differences in actual test administration, such as the behavior of proctors. The effects of some of these differences can be large. Aggregated scores from embedded material could also be biased by differences in the inclusion of students with disabilities or limited proficiency in English, as well as other differences in the percentages of students actually tested.

Other impediments stem from the nature of the embedded material itself. When only modest amounts of material from a test are embedded, the resulting scores are likely to be unreliable. Moreover, modest selections of material from the national test may fail to represent the national test adequately, which could bias interpretations of performance on the embedded material. This bias would likely affect some individuals and states more than others. We agree with the conclusions in *Uncommon Measures* (National Research Council, 1999c) that statistical linkage will not suffice to overcome the limited amount and likely unrepresentativeness of embedded test materials. As differences in emphasis among tests are reduced, this fundamental obstacle will shrink, but so will the need for embedding.

It is important to note that while some of these impediments to obtaining adequate scores are tractable, others are not. For example, states could time their own assessments to match the timing of the national assessment that is the source of embedded material, to resolve problems stemming from differences in timing. But differences in use, motivation, and test security could prove insurmountable obstacles to providing comparable scores.

Another threat to inferences based on embedding is particularly important in an era of test-based accountability: the likely changes over time in the relationship between the state and the national test. In *Uncommon Measures* (National Research Council, 1999c), this problem was discussed in terms of the instability of linkages, but it extends beyond linking and can affect inferences from embedded material even in the absence of statistical linkage. To some extent, this problem may arise even in the absence of high stakes: for example, changes in student populations, unintended and intended changes in the design of assessments, and other unmeasured factors may cause a shift in the scale of measurement, so that it becomes either easier or harder to attain a given score. However, high stakes may greatly increase the instability of any concordance between the state and national tests. Under such circumstances, assuming that the performance on embedded material has a stable relationship to performance on the parts of the national test that are not administered would lead to biased estimates of performance gains.

Criterion-referenced inferences pose a particular difficulty for embedding. Criterion-referenced conclusions, including those expressed in terms of performance standards such as the NAEP achievement levels, entail inferences about the specific knowledge and skills that students exhibit at each performance level. To the extent that embedded material is abridged or unrepresentative of the national test, these inferences may be particularly difficult to support on the basis of performance on the embedded material.

Because of the large number of obstacles to success and the intractability of some of them, the committee does not offer recommendations for making these forms of embedding more successful. Rather, the committee concludes that under most circumstances, embedding should not be used as a method of estimating scores for individual students on a national test that is not fully administered.

Under certain circumstances, however, an alternate approach may provide adequate national scores.

> **CONCLUSION 2:** When a national test designed to produce individual scores is administered in its entirety and under standard conditions that are the same from state to state and consistent with its standardization, it can provide a national common measure. States may separately administer custom-developed, state items close in time with the national test and use student responses to both the state items and selected national test items to calculate a state score. This approach provides both national and state scores for individual students and may reduce students' testing burdens relative to the administration of two overlapping tests.

This approach assumes that the state items are neither physically embedded in the national test nor administered at precisely the same time and therefore will not generate context effects that alter performance on the national test. It differs from the situation discussed above in several key respects. Because the national assessment is administered completely and under standard conditions, many of the threats to comparability of national scores—such as context effects, differences in timing, and differences in administration—may be avoided.

It is important to note, however, that this approach does have limitations. It becomes less and less efficient as differences between the national test and state standards and test specifications grow larger. It provides a national measure only for states that use the same national test; different national tests can provide results that are not comparable. Moreover, depending on the design of the assessment and the uses to which it is put, it is vulnerable to some other threats to comparability, such as inflation of scores from coaching and bias from differences in the exclusion of low-scoring groups. If administrative conditions differ, performance on the national items that contribute to state scores could be different than it would be if they were administered with the state items. The committee did not deliberate about the effects of this approach on the quality of state scores.

CONCLUSION 3: Although embedding appears to offer gains in efficiency relative to administering two tests and does reduce student testing time, in practice it is often complex and burdensome and may compromise test security.

The relative efficiency of embedding must be evaluated on a case-by-case basis and depends on many factors, including the length of the embedded test, required changes in administration practices at the state level, and differing regulations about which students are tested or excluded. In addition, states must weigh the costs and benefits that are associated with any embedding approach.

The committee was able in the time available to consider only briefly the use of embedding to obtain aggregated information rather than to obtain information about individual students. Thus, we do not offer a conclusion on such uses, but rather, a tentative finding. It appears that under some conditions and for some purposes, it may be possible to use embedding to support conclusions other than those pertaining to the performance of individual students. For example, embedding may be a feasible means of benchmarking state standards to national standards in terms of difficulty. That is, it may be practical to find out through embedding whether a state's standards are comparable in difficulty to a set of national standards. This is a relatively undemanding inference, however, because it does not necessarily imply that the state and national assessments are actually measuring similar things or that the particular individuals or schools that score well on one would consistently score well on the other. In other words, it does not entail estimating performance on the national test that is not fully administered.

The extent to which embedding would provide valid estimates of aggregated national scores of groups of students—such as schools, districts, or states—on a national test that is not fully administered remains uncertain. Aggregation does lessen the effects of certain types of measurement error that contribute to the unreliability of scores for individual students. Many of the impediments to embedding discussed by the committee, however, vary systematically among groups, such as differences in rules for the use of accommodations and differences in the contexts provided by state tests, and aggregation will not alleviate the distortions caused by these factors.

References

American Educational Research Association, American Psychological Association, and National Council on Measurement in Education

    1985   *Standards for Educational and Psychological Testing.* Washington, DC: American Psychological Association.

    in   *Standards for Educational and Psychological Testing.* Washington, DC: American Educational Research Association.
    press

American Institutes for Research

    1998a   Background Paper Reviewing Laws and Regulations, Current Practice, and Research Relevant to Inclusion and Accommodations for Students with Disabilities. Prepared for the National Assessment Governing Board in Support of Contract RJ97153001. Palo Alto, CA, November 6.

    1998b   Background Paper Reviewing Laws and Regulations, Current Practice, and Research Relevant to Inclusion and Accommodations for Students with Limited English Proficiency. Prepared for the National Assessment Governing Board in Support of Contract RJ97153001. Palo Alto, CA, November 6.

Beaton, A.E., and E.J. Gonzales

    1995   *The NAEP Primer.* Chestnut Hill, MA: Center for the Study of Testing, Evaluation, and Educational Policy, Boston College.

Beaton, A.E., and R. Zwick

    1992   Overview of the National Assessment of Educational Progress. *Journal of Educational Statistics* 17:95-109.

Beggs, D.L., and A.N. Hieronymus

    1968   Uniformity of growth in the basic skills throughout the school year and during the summer. *Journal of Educational Measurement* 5:91-97.

Bock, D., and M. Zimowski
  1999   Memo to Don McLaughlin, AIR, in reference to Linking Report No. 2. Un-published document. National Opinion Research Center, University of Chicago.
Brennan, R.L.
  1992   The context of context effects. *Applied Measurement in Education* 5(3):225-264.
Childs, R., and R. Hill
  1998   Proposed Analysis of NAEP Data for Louisiana. Draft paper. National Center for the Improvement of Educational Assessment, Inc., Dover, NH.
Cooper, H., B. Nye, C. Kelly, J. Lindsay, and S. Greathouse
  1996   The effects of summer vacation on achievement test scores: A narrative and meta-analytic review. *Review of Educational Research* 66:227-268.
CTB/McGraw-Hill
  1997   *Terra Nova: Technical Bulletin 1*. Monterey, CA: CTB/McGraw-Hill.
Donahue, P.L., K.E. Voelkl, J.R. Campbell, and J. Mazzeo
  1999   NAEP 1998 Reading Report Card for the Nation and the States. Office of Educational Research and Improvement, National Center for Education Statistics. Washington, DC: U.S. Department of Education.
Dulmage, H.G.
  1993   The Effect of Increasing Testing Time on the Results of the Reading Comprehension and Reference Materials Subtests of the Iowa Test of Basic Skills. DAI, Vol. 54-5A, p. 1608. Unpublished doctoral dissertation, Michigan State University.
Dunbar, S.B., D.M. Koretz, and H.D. Hoover
  1991   Quality control in the development and use of performance assessment. *Applied Measurement in Education* 4(4):289-303.
Faggen, J., and M. McPeek
  1981   Practice Effects for Four Different Item Types. Paper presented at the National Council on Measurement in Education Annual Meeting, Los Angeles, CA.
Feldt, L.S., R.A. Forsyth, T.N. Ansley, and S.D. Alnot
  1996   *Iowa Test of Educational Development, Form M: Norms and Score Conversions with Technical Information*. Chicago: Riverside Publishing.
Frederiksen, N.
  1984   The real test bias: Influences of testing on teaching and learning. *American Psychologist* 39:193-202.
Gulliksen, H.O.
  1950   *Theory of Mental Tests*. New York: John Wiley and Sons.
Halla, J.W.
  1988   A Psychological Study of Psychometric Differences in Graduate Record Examination Test Scores Between Learning Disabled and Non-Learning Disabled Adults. DAI, Vol. 49-11A, p. 3341. Unpublished doctoral dissertation, Texas Tech University.

Hambleton, R.K., R.M. Jaeger, D.M. Koretz, J. Millman, and S.E. Phillips
1995   *Review of the Measurement Quality of the Kentucky Instructional Results Information System, 1991-1994.* Frankfort, KY: Office of Educational Accountability, Kentucky General Assembly.

Harcourt Brace Educational Measurement
1997   *Stanford Achievement Test, Ninth Edition: Technical Data Report.* San Antonio, TX: Harcourt Brace Educational Measurement.

Hartka, E., and D. McLaughlin
1994   A study of the administration of the 1992 National Assessment of Educational Progress trial state assessment. Pp. 479-522 in *The Trial State Assessment: Prospects and Realities: Background Studies*, National Academy of Education Panel on the Evaluation of the NAEP Trial State Assessment: 1992 Trial State Assessment. Stanford, CA: National Academy of Education, Stanford University.

Hoff, D.J.
1998   Achieve declares itself ready to aid states with reforms. *Education Week* 18(9):6.
1999   Achieve planning new math test for 8th grade. *Education Week* 18(21):16.

Hoover, H.D., A.N. Hieronymus, D.A. Frisbie, and S.B. Dunbar
1996   *Iowa Tests of Basic Skills, Form M: Norms and Score Conversions With Technical Information.* Chicago: Riverside Publishing.

Horne, L.V., and M.K. Garty
1981   What the Test Score Really Reflects: Observations of Teacher Behavior During Standardized Achievement Test Administration. Paper presented at the American Educational Research Association Annual Meeting. Los Angeles, CA.

Huesman, R.L.
1999   The Validity of the ITBS Reading Comprehension Test Scores for Learning Disabled and Non-Learning Disabled Students Under Extended-Time Conditions. Unpublished doctoral disertation, University of Iowa.

Iowa Testing Programs
1999   Comparisons of Iowa Median Midyear Performance. Unpublished internal document, Iowa Testing Programs, University of Iowa.

Jakwerth, P.R., F.B. Stancavage, and E.D. Reed
1999   An Investigation of Why Students Do Not Respond to Questions. Report commissioned by the NAEP Validity Studies Panel, American Institutes for Research, Washington, DC.

Joseph, R.M.
1998   The Effects of the Accommodation of Extended Time Limits on the CAT-5 for Middle School-Aged Individuals With Dyslexia. DAI, Vol. 59-3A, p. 772. Unpublished doctoral dissertation, University of Lowell.

Journal of Educational Measurement
1992   Special Issue: The National Assessment of Educational Progress 29(2). J. Algina, ed.

Journal of Educational Statistics
1992   Special Issue: National Assessment of Educational Progress 17(2). R. Zwick, guest ed.

Kimmel, E.W.
  1997   Unintended Consequences of Testing the Integrity of Teachers and Students.
            Paper presented at the National Conference on Large Scale Assessment,
            Colorado Springs, CO.

Kiplinger, V.L., and R.L. Linn
  1996   Raising the stakes of test administration: The impact on student perfor-
            mance on the National Assessment of Educational Progress. *Educational As-
            sessment* 3(2):111-133.

Koretz, D.M., and S.I. Barron
  1998   *The Validity of Gains in Scores on the Kentucky Instructional Results Information
            System (KIRIS)*. Washington, DC: RAND.

Koretz, D.M., B. Stecher, S.P. Klein, and D. McCaffrey
  1994   The Vermont Portfolio Assessment Program: Findings and implications. *Edu-
            cational Measurement: Issues and Practice* 13(3):5-16.

Koretz, D.M., S.I. Barron, K. Mitchell, and B. Stecher
  1996a   *The Perceived Effects of the Kentucky Instructional Results Information System
            (KIRIS)*. MR-792-PCT/FF. Santa Monica, CA: RAND.

Koretz, D.M., K. Mitchell, S.I. Barron, and S. Keith
  1996b   *The Perceived Effects of the Maryland School Performance Assessment Program*.
            CSE Technical Report No. 409. Los Angeles: Center for the Study of Evalu-
            ation, Universty of California.

Kronholz, J.
  1998   States take lead in national tests for schoolchildren. *Wall Street Journal* Dec.
            23:A16.

Leary, L.F., and N.J. Dorans
  1985   Implications for Altering the Context in Which Test Items Appear: A His-
            torical Perspective on an Immediate Concern. *Review of Educational Research*
            55(3):387-413.

Ligon, G.
  1985   Opportunity Knocked Out: Reducing Cheating by Teachers on Student
            Tests. Paper presented at the American Educational Research Association
            Annual Meeting, Chicago, IL.

Linn, R.L.
  1993a   *Educational Measurement*. Third Edition. Phoenix, AZ: Oryx Press.
  1993b   Linking results of distinct assessments. *Applied Measurement in Education*
            6(1):83-102.

Martin, M.O. and D.L. Kelly, eds.
  1996   *Third International Mathematics and Science Study Technical Report Volume I:
            Design and Development*. Chestnut Hill, MA: Center for the Study of Test-
            ing, Evaluation, and Educational Policy, Boston College.

Mazzeo, J., J. Donoghue, and C. Hombo
  1999   Memo to Pascal D. Forgione, Commisioner of Education Statistics, NCES;
            Re: A Summary of Initial Analyses of 1998 State NAEP Exclusion Rates.
            Available online: http://nces.ed.gov/pressrelease/naep599ets.html (6/15/99).

McLaughlin, D.
    1998   Study of the Linkages of 1996 NAEP and State Mathematics Assessments in Four States: Final Report. Draft unpublished paper. John C. Flanagan Research Center, American Institutes for Research, Education Statistics Services Institute.

Musick, M.D.
    1996   Setting Education Standards High Enough. Unpublished paper. Southern Regional Education Board, Atlanta.

National Research Council
    1997   *Educating One and All: Students With Disabilities and Standards-Based Reform.* Committee on Goals 2000 and the Inclusion of Students with Disabilities. L. M. McDonnell, M. J. McLaughlin, and P. Morison, eds. Board on Testing and Assessment, Commission on Behavioral and Social Sciences and Education. Washington, DC: National Academy Press.

    1999a   *Grading the Nation's Report Card: Evaluating NAEP and Transforming the Assessment of Educational Assessment.* Committee on the Evaluation of National and State Assessments of Educational Progress. J.W. Pellegrino, L.R. Jones, and K.M. Mitchell, eds. Board on Testing and Assessment, Commission on Behavioral and Social Sciences and Education. Washington, DC: National Academy Press.

    1999b   *High Stakes: Testing for Tracking, Promotion, and Graduation.* Committee on Appropriate Test Use. J.P. Heubert and R.M. Hauser, eds. Board on Testing and Assessment, Commission on Behavioral and Social Sciences and Education. Washington, DC: National Academy Press.

    1999c   *Uncommon Measures: Equivalence and Linkage Among Educational Tests.* Committee the Equivalency and Linkage of Educational Tests. M.J. Feuer, P.W. Holland, B.F. Green, M.W. Bertenthal, and F.C. Hemphill, eds. Board on Testing and Assessment, Commission on Behavioral and Social Sciences and Education. Washington, DC: National Academy Press.

Nolen, S.B., T.M. Haladyna, and N.S. Haas
    1992   Uses and abuses of achievement test scores. *Educational Measurement: Issues and Practice* 11(2):9-15.

Olson, J.F., L. Bond, and C. Andrews
    in   *Annual Survey of State Student Assessment Programs: Fall 1998.* Washington,
    press   DC: Council of Chief State School Officers.

O'Neil, H.F., B. Sugrue, J. Abedi, E.L. Baker, and S. Golan
    1992   *Final Report of Experimental Studies on Motivation and NAEP Test Performance.* Los Angeles, CA: Center for Research, Evaluation, Standards, and Student Testing.

Roeber, E., L. Bond, and S. Connealy
    1998   *Annual Survey of State Student Assessment Programs: Fall 1997.* Washington, DC: Council of Chief State School Officers.

Rudman, H.C., and S.W. Raudenbush
    1996   The Effect of Exceeding Prescribed Time Limits in the Administration of Standardized Achievement Tests. Paper presented at the National Council on Measurement in Education Annual Meeting, New York City.

Shavelson, R.J., G.P. Baxter, and X. Gao
    1993   Sampling variability of performance assessments. *Journal of Educational Measurement* 30(3):215-232.
U.S. Congress
    1998   *Conference Report on H.R. 4328, Omnibus Consolidated Appropriations Act for FY 1999.* Washington, DC: U.S. Government Printing Office.
U.S. General Accounting Office
    1998   *Student Testing: Issues Related to Voluntary National Mathematics and Reading Tests.* GAO/HEHS-98-163. Washington, DC: U.S. Government Printing Office.
Whitney, D.R., and W.M. Patience
    1981   *Work Rates on the GED Tests: Relationships With Examinee Age and Test Time Limits.* Washington, DC: GED Testing Service, American Council on Education.
Williams, E.B.
    1981   Performance of Inner City Learning Disabled and Emotionally Disturbed Youth on Power and Timed Achievement Tests. DAI, Vol. 41-12A, p. 5063. Unpublished doctoral dissertation, University of Connecticut.
Wolf, L.F., J.K. Smith, and M.E. Birnbaum
    1995   Consequence of performance, test motivation, and mentally taxing items. *Applied Measurement in Education* 8(4):341-351.

Glossary

This glossary provides definitions of technical terms and concepts used in this report. Note that technical usage may differ from common usage. For many of the terms, multiple definitions can be found in the literature. Words set in *italics* are defined elsewhere in the glossary.

Accommodation A change in the standard procedure for administering a *test* or in the mode of response required of examinees, used to lessen *bias* in the *scores* of individuals with a special need or disability. Examples of accommodations include allotting extra time and providing the *test* in large type.

Achievement levels Descriptions of student or adult competency in a particular subject area, usually defined as ordered categories on a continuum, often labeled from "basic" to "advanced," that constitute broad ranges for classifying performance. The National Assessment of Educational Progress (*NAEP*) defines three achievement levels for each subject and grade being assessed: basic, proficient, and advanced. The National Assessment Governing Board (NAGB), the governing body for *NAEP*, describes the knowledge and skills demonstrated by students at or above each of these three levels of achievement, and provides exemplars of performance for each. NAGB also reports the percentage of students who are in the four categories of achievement defined by the three levels, basic, proficient, or advanced. NAGB does not provide a description for the below basic category.

Assessment   Any systematic method of obtaining evidence from *tests* and collateral sources used to draw inferences about characteristics of people, objects, or programs for a specific purpose; often used interchangeably with *test*.

Bias   In a test, a *systematic error* in a *test score*. Bias usually favors one group of *test* takers over another.

Calibration   (1) With respect to scales, the process of setting a *test score* scale, including the *mean, standard deviation*, and possibly the shape of the *score distribution*, so that *scores* on the scale have the same relative meaning as *scores* on a related *score* scale. (2) With respect to *items*, the process of determining the relation of *item* responses to the underlying scale that the *item* is measuring, including indications of an *item*'s difficulty, correlation to the scale, and susceptibility to guessing.

Common measure   A scale of measurement that has a single meaning. *Scores* from *tests* that are calibrated (see *calibration*) to this scale support the same inferences about student performance from one locality to another and from one year to the next.

Constructed-response item   An exercise for which examinees must create their own responses or products rather than choose a response from an enumerated set. See *selected-response item*.

Content domain   The set of behaviors, knowledge, skills, abilities, attitudes ,or other characteristics measured by a test, represented in a detailed specification, and often organized into categories by which *items* are classified.

Distribution   The number, or the percentage, of cases having each possible data value on a scale of data values. Distributions are often reported in terms of grouped ranges of data values. In testing, data values are usually *test scores*. A distribution can be characterized by its *mean* and *standard deviation*.

Domain The full array of a particular subject matter being addressed by an *assessment.*

Effect size A measure of the practical effect of a statistical difference, usually a difference of the *means* of two *distributions.* The *mean* difference between two *distributions,* or an equivalent difference, is expressed in units of the *standard deviation* of the dominant *distribution* or of some average of the two *standard deviations.* For example, if two *distributions* had *means* of 50 and 54, and both had *standard deviations* of 10, the effect size of their *mean* difference would be 4/10, or 0.4. The effect size is sometimes called the standardized mean difference. In other contexts, other ways are sometimes used to express the practical size of an observed statistical difference.

Embedding In testing, including all or part of one *test* in another. The embedded part may be kept together as a unit or interspersed throughout the test.

Equating The process of statistical adjustments by which the *scores* on two or more alternate *forms* are placed on a common scale. The process assumes that the *test forms* have been constructed to the same explicit content and statistical specifications and administered under identical procedures.

Field test A *test* administration used to check the adequacy of testing procedures, generally including *test* administration, *test* responding, *test* scoring, and *test* reporting.

Form In testing, a particular *test* in a set of *tests,* all of which have the same *test specifications* and are mutually equated.

Framework The detailed description of the *test domain* in the way that it will be represented by a test.

High-stakes test A *test* whose results have important, direct consequences for examinees, programs, or institutions tested.

Item   A generic term used to refer to a question or an exercise on a *test* or *assessment*. The *test* taker must respond to the item in some way. Since many *test* questions have the grammatical form of a statement, the neutral term item is preferred.

Item format   The form in which a question is posed on a *test* and the form in which the response is to be made. The formats include, among others, *selected-response items* (multiple-choice) and *constructed-response items*, which may be either short-answer or extended-response *items*.

Item pool   The aggregate of *items* from which a test's *items* are selected during *test development* or the total set of *items* from which a particular *test* is selected for a test taker during adaptive testing.

Limited English proficiency (LEP)   A term used to identify students whose performance on *tests* of achievement may be inappropriately low because of their poor proficiency in English.

Linking   Placing two or more *tests* on the same scale so that *scores* can be used interchangeably.

Matrix sampling   A measurement format in which a large set of *test items* is organized into a number of relatively short *item* sets, each of which is randomly assigned to a subsample of *test* takers, thereby avoiding the need to administer all *items* to all examinees.

Measurement error   The amount of variation in a measured value, such as a *score*, due to unknown, random factors. In testing, measurement error is viewed as the difference between an observed *score* and a corresponding theoretical true *score* or proficiency.

Metric   The units in which the values on a scale are expressed.

Norm-referenced   Interpreted by comparison with the performance of those in a specified population. A norm-referenced *test score* is interpreted on the basis of a comparison of a *test* taker's performance to the performance of other people in a specified reference population, or by a comparison of a group to other groups. See *criterion-referenced.*

Norms Statistics or tabular data that summarize the *distribution* of *test* performance for one or more specified groups, such as *test* takers of various ages or grades. Norms are usually designed to represent some larger population, such as all test takers in the country.

Performance standard An objective definition of a certain level of performance in some *domain* in terms of a *cut-score* or a range of *scores* on the *score* scale of a *test* measuring proficiency in that *domain*. Also, sometimes, a statement or description of a set of operational tasks exemplifying a level of performance associated with a more general *content standard*; the statement may be used to guide judgments about the location of a *cut-score* on a *score* scale.

Proficiency levels See *achievement levels*.

Reliability The degree to which the *scores* are consistent over repeated applications of a measurement procedure and hence are dependable, and repeatable; the degree to which *scores* are free of errors of measurement. Reliability is usually expressed by a unit-free index that either is, or resembles, a product-moment correlation. In classical *test* theory, the term represents the ratio of true *score variance* to observed *score variance* for a particular examinee population. The conditions under which the coefficient is estimated may involve variation in *test* forms, measurement occasions, raters, or scorers, and may entail multiple examinee products or performances. These and other variations in conditions give rise to qualifying adjectives, such as alternate-forms reliability, internal-consistency reliability, *test*-retest reliability, etc.

Scale score A *score* on a *test* that is expressed on some defined scale of measurement.

Score Any specific number resulting from the *assessment* of an individual; a generic term applied for convenience to such diverse measures as *test scores*, production counts, absence records, course grades, ratings, and so forth.

Selected-response item *Test item* for which *test* taker selects response from provided choices; also known as a multiple-choice *item*. See *constructed-response item*.

Standard deviation   An index of the degree to which a set of data values is concentrated about its *mean*. Sometimes referred to as "spread." The standard deviation measures the variability in a *distribution* of quantities. *Distributions* with relatively small standard deviations are relatively concentrated; larger standard deviations signify greater variability. In common *distributions*, like the mathematically defined "normal *distribution*," roughly 67 percent of the quantities are within (plus or minus) 1 standard deviation from the *mean*; about 95 percent are within (plus or minus) 2 standard deviations; nearly all are within (plus or minus) 3 standard deviations. See *distribution, effect size, variance.*

Standardization   In *test* administration, maintaining a constant testing environment and conducting the *test* according to detailed rules and specifications so that testing conditions are the same for all *test* takers. In statistical analysis, transforming a variable so that its *standard deviation* is 1.0 for some specified population or sample.

Systematic error   A *score* component (often observed indirectly), not related to the characteristic being measured, that appears to be related to some salient variable or subgrouping of cases in an analysis. See *bias*.

Test   A set of *items* given under prescribed and standardized conditions for the purpose of measuring the knowledge, skill, or ability of a person. The person's responses to the *items* yield a *score*, which is a numerical evaluation of the person's performance on the test.

Test development   The process through which a *test* is planned, constructed, evaluated, and modified, including consideration of the content, format, administration, scoring, *item* properties, *scaling*, and technical quality for its intended purpose.

Test specifications   A *framework* that specifies the proportion of *items* that assess each content and process or skill area; the format of *items*, responses, and scoring protocols and procedures; and the desired psychometric properties of the *items* and test, such as the *distribution* of *item* difficulty and discrimination indices.

Validity   An overall evaluation of the degree to which accumulated evidence and theory support specific interpretations of *test scores*.

Biographical Sketches of
Committee Members and Staff

DANIEL M. KORETZ (*Chair*) is a professor of educational research, measurement, and evaluation at Boston College and a senior social scientist at RAND Education in Washington, DC. His research focuses on educational assessment and explores both the quality of assessments and their effects on schooling. He has carried out extensive work with the National Assessment of Educational Progress (NAEP) and is currently directing a study of the variability of performance in seven countries in the Third International Mathematics and Science Study. Dr. Koretz received his Ph.D. in developmental psychology from Cornell University.

SUSAN A. AGRUSO is director of the Office of Assessment of the South Carolina Department of Education. In that capacity she is responsible for development, pilot testing, and administration of the state's educational testing program. Her research interests focus on the development of alternative assessment measures, the alignment of educational standards, assessments, and instructional practices, and gender and equity issues in testing. Dr. Agruso earned her Ph.D. in instructional psychology from the University of New York at Albany.

MERYL W. BERTENTHAL (*Study Director*) is a senior program officer in the Board on Testing and Assessment of the National Research Council. Previously, she served as a senior research associate with the Committee on Equivalency and Linkage of Educational Tests, also with the Board on Testing and Assessment. Her areas of interest include student assessment, educational reform, and education policy. Ms. Bertenthal earned her M.A.Ed from Clark University and completed a post master's degree program in counseling education at the University of Virginia.

BERT F. GREEN is a professor of psychology, emeritus, at Johns Hopkins University. He is a member of a national committee that is revising the standards for educational and psychological testing. He serves on the psychometric council for the School Performance Assessment Program of the Maryland State Department of Education. His research concerns psychometric methods for computer-based adaptive testing, as well as performance assessment and health assessment. Dr. Green earned his Ph.D. in psychology from Princeton University.

RONALD K. HAMBLETON is distinguished university professor and chair of the Research and Evaluation Methods Program at the University of Massachusetts at Amherst. His current research includes work on item response theory (IRT) model fit, optimal test design, differential item functioning, computer-adaptive testing, test translations and adaptations, problems associated with score reporting and standard-setting, reliability assessment on credentialing exams, and validity issues associated with performance assessments in education and the credentialing field. Dr. Hambleton received his Ph.D. in psychometric methods and statistics from the University of Toronto.

PAUL W. HOLLAND is a professor in the Graduate School of Education and the Department of Statistics at the University of California, Berkeley. He is a member of the Board on Testing and Assessment and served as the chair of the Committee on the Equivalency and Linkage of Educational Tests. He participates in the Berkeley Evaluation and Assessment Research Project, working on developing new assessment techniques and evaluation methodologies for practical application in the schools. He also serves on a technical advisory committee for the California Learning Assessment System (CLAS). Dr. Holland earned his Ph.D. in statistics from Stanford University.

H.D. HOOVER is a professor of statistics and educational measurement at the University of Iowa, director of the Iowa Basic Skills Testing Program, and senior author of the Iowa Test of Basic Skills. His research interests include test scaling, test equating, group differences in item and test performance, and the measurement of mathematics achievement. Dr. Hoover received his Ph.D. in statistics and educational measurement from the University of Iowa.

BRIAN W. JUNKER is an associate professor of statistics at Carnegie Mellon University. His research has focused on latent variable models used in the design and analysis of standardized tests, small-scale experiments in psychology and psychiatry, and large-scale educational surveys such as the National Assessment of Educational Progress (NAEP). Dr. Junker received his Ph.D. in statistics from the University of Illinois.

JOHN J. SHEPHARD is a senior project assistant in the Board on Testing and Assessment of the National Research Council. In addition to his work with the Committee on Embedding Test Items in State and District Assessments, he works with the Committee on the Evaluation of National and State Assessments of Educational Progress and the recently formed Committee on Programs for Advanced Study of Mathematics and Science in American High Schools. Mr. Shephard received his B.A. in anthropology from The Colorado College.

JAMES A. WATTS is vice president for state services at the Southern Regional Education Board (SREB). He coordinates the board's work with the region's 15 state governors, legislatures, and their staff. Among his substantive interests are educational standards and accountability, school leadership, and school reform. Dr. Watts received his Ed.D. in educational administration and public policy from Indiana University.

KAREN K. WIXSON is a professor and the interim dean of the School of Education at the University of Michigan. Her areas of expertise include the development of curriculum and instructional methodology for teaching reading, as well as the design and construction of assessment tools to measure reading achievement. She has done considerable work related to the development of the National Assessment of Educational Progress reading tests and served as an adviser for the Voluntary National Tests for 4th-grade reading. Dr. Wixson received her Ph.D. in reading education from Syracuse University.

WENDY M. YEN is vice president of research at CTB/McGraw-Hill.

Her research interests include scaling and equating. She is past president of the National Council on Measurement in Education and has served as a trustee of the Psychometric Society. She currently serves on the editorial advisory boards of the *Journal of Educational Measurement* and *Applied Measurement in Education* and recently served as a consultant to the NRC Committee on the Equivalence and Linkage of Educational Tests. She received her Ph.D. from the University of California at Berkeley.

REBECCA ZWICK is a professor of education and director of the research methodology program in the Graduate School of Education at the University of California at Santa Barbara. Her current work includes the refinement and application of methods she and her colleagues have developed for assessing differential item functioning (item bias) in small samples, as well as a book for the general public on the use of standardized testing in college and graduate school admissions. She received her M.S. in statistics from Rutgers University and her Ph.D. in quantitative methods in education from the University of California at Berkley.